Indian English

Pingali Sailaja

Edinburgh University Press

To
Bhagavan

© Pingali Sailaja, 2009

Transferred to digital print 2012

Edinburgh University Press Ltd
22 George Square, Edinburgh

www.euppublishing.com

Typeset in 10.5/12 Janson
by Servis Filmsetting Ltd, Stockport, Cheshire

A CIP record for this book is available from the British Library

ISBN 978 0 7486 2594 9 (hardback)
ISBN 978 0 7486 2595 6 (paperback)

The right of Pingali Sailaja
to be identified as author of this work
has been asserted in accordance with
the Copyright, Designs and Patents Act 1988.

Published with the support of the Edinburgh University Scholarly
Publishing Initiatives Fund.

Indian English

Dialects of English

Series Editors:
Joan Beal (University of Sheffield)
Patrick Honeybone (University of Edinburgh)
April McMahon (University of Edinburgh)

Advisory Board:
Laurie Bauer (Victoria University of Wellington)
Jenny Cheshire (Queen Mary, University of London)
Karen Corrigan (University of Newcastle upon Tyne)
Heinz Giegerich (University of Edinburgh)
Peter L. Patrick (University of Essex)
Peter Trudgill (University of Fribourg, UEA, Agder UC, La Trobe University)
Walt Wolfram (North Carolina State University)

Volumes available in the series:
Robert McColl Millar, *Northern and Insular Scots*
978 0 7486 2317 4

David Deterding, *Singapore English*
978 0 7486 2545 1

Jennifer Hay, Margaret Maclagan and Elizabeth Gordon, *New Zealand English*
978 0 7486 2530 7

Pingali Sailaja, *Indian English*
978 0 7486 2595 6

Forthcoming titles include:
Bridget L. Anderson, *Smoky Mountain English*
978 0 7486 3039 4

Sandra Clarke, *Newfoundland English*
978 0 7486 2617 5

Karen Corrigan, *Northern Irish English*
978 0 7486 3429 3

Contents

Preface		viii
Acknowledgements		ix
Abbreviations, Symbols and other Notational Conventions Used		x

1	Introduction		1
	1.1	Geography	1
	1.2	Demography	2
	1.3	Official status	4
	1.4	Domains of use	5
	1.5	Cultural factors	6
	1.6	'Indian English' versus 'English in India'	13
2	Phonetics and Phonology		17
	2.1	Consonant sounds	19
		2.1.1 /r/	19
		2.1.2 /v/ and /w/ or /ʋ/	20
		2.1.3 /θ/ and /ð/ or /t̪, t̪h/, /d̪/	21
		2.1.4 /t/ and /d/ or /ʈ/ and /ɖ/	21
		2.1.5 The other consonants	22
		2.1.6 Non-contrastive sounds	22
	2.2	Vowel sounds	24
		2.2.1 The short vowels	24
		2.2.2 The long vowels	25
		2.2.3 Diphthongs	25
	2.3	Other aspects of segments	26
		2.3.1 Spelling pronunciation	26
		2.3.2 Some specific words	27
		2.3.3 Morphophonology	28
		2.3.4 Simplification of consonant clusters	29
	2.4	Suprasegmental features	29
		2.4.1 Stress	29
		2.4.2 Rhythm and intonation	34

		2.4.3	Other aspects of connected speech	36
	2.5	Variation in individual speakers		37
3	Morphosyntax			39
	3.1	Indian English – British or American?		40
	3.2	Verbs		43
		3.2.1	Verb complements	43
		3.2.2	Verb particles	47
		3.2.3	The progressive	48
		3.2.4	Tense concord (absent)	49
		3.2.5	Auxiliary verbs	50
	3.3	Articles		51
	3.4	Topicalisation		53
	3.5	*only*		55
	3.6	Question formation		56
		3.6.1	*Wh-* questions	56
		3.6.2	*Yes-no* questions	58
		3.6.3	Tag questions	59
	3.7	Reduplication, reduced phrases, fused phrases		59
	3.8	Prepositions		61
	3.9	Idioms		61
	3.10	Code-switching		62
	3.11	Inflectional forms		63
4	Lexis and Discourse			66
	4.1	Indian English lexis		66
		4.1.1	British, American and Indian	66
		4.1.2	Indian meanings	68
	4.2	Indian influence on English		69
		4.2.1	Assimilated items	69
		4.2.2	Restricted items	72
	4.3	Lexical innovations		75
		4.3.1	Compounding	76
		4.3.2	Hybrid constructions	80
		4.3.3	Affixation	80
		4.3.4	Abbreviations, clippings and acronyms	82
		4.3.5	Redundancy	84
	4.4	Discourse features and other strategies of communication		85
		4.4.1	Linkers	85
		4.4.2	Address forms	86
		4.4.3	Welcoming and goodbyes	87
	4.5	Aspects of politeness		88

	4.6	Code-switching with Indian languages	91
	4.7	Style	93
5	History and Changes in Progress	95
	5.1	History	96
		5.1.1 The pre-British period (1498–1600)	96
		5.1.2 The pre-Macaulay period (1600–1835)	97
		5.1.3 The pre-independence period (1835–1947): The institutionalisation of English education	106
		5.1.4 The post-independence period (1947–2006)	110
	5.2	Indian English pidgins	112
	5.3	Changes in progress	115
		5.3.1 Spelling	115
		5.3.2 Other linguistic aspects	117
6	Survey of Previous Work and Annotated Bibliography	120
	6.1	Comprehensive/general works and bibliographies	120
	6.2	Phonetics and phonology	124
	6.3	Morphosyntax	125
	6.4	Discourse, lexis, lexicons and glossaries	126
	6.5	History, education and politics	129
	6.6	Samples and corpora	131
7	Sample Texts	133
	7.1	Literature	133
	7.2	Official documents and other letters	137
	7.3	Newspaper articles and reports	141
	7.4	Letters to the editor	146
	7.5	Advertisements	149
	7.6	Miscellaneous	152
	7.7	Lectures	154
	7.8	Audio samples	156

Bibliography of Cited Works 159
Index 169

Preface

This volume is a description of English as it is spoken and used in India. The volume focuses mostly on those features that are pan-Indian. Regional differences are touched upon, to some extent, where relevant. Since India is a country of continental proportions, as the cliché goes, it is not possible to cover every linguistic detail or the variation across all the regions. The book focuses on the more important or common features in evidence across the country. Indian English is classified in this book as standard, non-standard and informal and features of these form the core of the book. At the same time, the attempt has been to cover standard Indian English as much as possible. One chapter deals with history and presents the events that led to the institutionalisation of English in India. The first chapter provides the context and current position of this language especially in relation to the cultural factors of the country.

This work is meant for students who are just beginning to be familiar with linguistic terminology. It is also a book meant for people who may be generally interested in language and (Indian) English. Since both these groups of readers are likely to be unfamiliar with terminology, it has been kept to a minimum. Every attempt has been made to keep the description simple and accessible. Where terminology and phonetic symbols have been unavoidable, they have been explained. At the same time, the book is likely to be of interest to specialists who are interested in Indian English. Those who would like to go beyond this work can make use of the chapter that gives details about some of the more important works in specific areas.

Much of the work already done on Indian English has touched on specific regional aspects. Some linguistic features have not been researched at all or not enough work has been done on them. This volume tries to provide a wide enough overview. It is hoped that the book will generate interest in researchers to take up more in-depth work on the different topics.

Acknowledgements

A number of people have contributed to the making of this book. I record my gratitude and appreciation here.

First, to Patrick Honeybone who gave me this opportunity to work on Indian English, and to the other editors of this series, April McMahon and Joan Beal, my thanks are due. Writing this book has been a tremendous learning process for me.

I further thank: Heinz Giegerich and Graeme Trousdale, for help from time to time; K. Narayana Chandran and M. Sridhar for sharing thoughts and material on English in India; Ranjit Pawar for doing audio recordings and particularly for the interview with Lou Hilt; Shree Deepa and Deepti Bhardwaj for help in conducting audio recordings in Hyderabad and Delhi; all the people who have provided the recordings and have given permission to put them up on the website; B. A. Prabhakar Babu for help in finding material related to phonetics; Mickey Suman and George Mathew for making interesting articles available to me; G. Govindaiah for hunting down elusive articles and without whose involvement this book would not have been completed on time; three batches of students with whom the matter that follows was discussed as a course; Y. Vasudev and Y. S. N. Murthy for technical assistance with the computer and their patience in explaining to me how things are to be done; R. Nagarajan for assistance with the chapter on samples; C. Venu Gopal for preparing the maps; Sarah Edwards and other staff of Edinburgh University Press for their prompt responses; the staff of the libraries in Hyderabad, Delhi, Calcutta, Bombay and London, where the research for this work was conducted, particularly to the staff of Asiatic Society, Bombay, and British Library; Richard Alford, of Charles Wallace India Trust, and British Council, for a timely research grant making a visit to the British Library in London possible.

Thanks also to my family and the many others, whose names may not be mentioned here but whom I remember, for contributions towards this book.

Abbreviations, Symbols and other Notational Conventions Used

AE	American English
BE	British English
IE	Indian English
RP	Received Pronunciation
SIEP	Standard Indian English Pronunciation
V	vowel
V:	long vowel
C	consonant
↘	falling tune
↗	rising tune
/.../	Encloses phonemic transcription
[...]	Encloses phonetic transcription
//	pause
'	in front of a syllable indicates a stressed syllable
*	in front of a form indicates that it is unacceptable

1 Introduction

Four hundred years after the first Englishman settled in India, followed by two hundred years of colonial rule and sixty years after Indian Independence, English emerges as the most visible legacy of the British. In the streets of all but the smaller villages, it is possible for perfect strangers to communicate, even if minimally, using this language.

1.1 Geography

India is the largest of all the countries in the Indian subcontinent, the other nations being Pakistan, Bangladesh, Nepal, Bhutan and Sri Lanka. India is surrounded by the sea on three sides – on the west by the Arabian Sea, on the east by the Bay of Bengal and on the south by the Indian Ocean. Sri Lanka, an island nation, is its closest neighbour in the south and it is separated from India by the Palk Strait. The north has a major boundary in the form of the mountain range of the Himalayas. In the north too are Nepal and Bhutan which are mountain nations. India is linked with Bangladesh on the east. In the north-east, it shares a boundary with Myanmar (erstwhile Burma). Pakistan lies to the west. In the Himalayas, India shares a boundary with China; the boundaries with Pakistan and China are disputed. With an area of 3.3 million square kilometres, India ranks as the seventh largest country in the world and second in Asia, after China (Government of India 2005). In this space are several perennial rivers, forests, mountain ranges, a desert and, with the long coastline, several beaches. Home to several religions, languages and cultural customs, India is an ancient civilisation and a land of immense diversity.

The country is administered through a loosely federal form of government and is organised into twenty-eight states and seven Union Territories, most of which are determined on a linguistic basis. Languages belong to four major families: Indo-Aryan, such as Hindi, Bengali, Marathi, Gujarati, Urdu; Tibeto-Burman, Angami, Ao, Bodo;

Austro-Asiatic or Munda, Santhali, Khasi; and Dravidian, Tamil, Telugu, Malayalam, Kannada.

In the heavily populated northern states of Uttar Pradesh, Bihar, Chhattisgarh, Haryana, Himachal Pradesh, Jharkhand, Uttarakhand and Madhya Pradesh, the various dialects of Hindi are spoken. The other major languages based on which the states are divided in the north are Punjabi, Kashmiri and Rajasthani.

In the east, the major languages are Bengali and Oriya. The northeastern part of the country consists of the following states, also called the Seven Sisters: Assam, Arunachal Pradesh, Mizoram, Manipur, Nagaland, Meghalaya and Tripura, whose languages belong to the Indo-Aryan, Austro-Asiatic and Tibeto-Burman groups.

In the west, the major languages are Marathi, Gujarati and Konkani. The south consists of four states and the major languages there belong to the Dravidian language family, which is distinct from those mentioned above.

Other languages that are not specifically associated with a state are Urdu, Sindhi, Nepali (Indo-Aryan) and Tulu (Dravidian).

1.2 Demography

Given India's vast population, the figures relating to languages are very impressive. In the statistics presented in this section, what emerges is the tremendous, even disproportionate, significance that English carries.

According to current estimates, the Indian population stands at about 1,125 million ('Population watch' 2007). With 2.4% of the world's surface, India bears 16.7% of the world's population (Government of India 2005). The 2001 Census of India reveals that 27.78% of India's population lives in urban areas – the urban figure is therefore in excess of 285 million people, including estimated figures for areas where census details could not be collected due to various reasons. The rest of India's population lives in rural areas (Registrar General and Census Commissioner 2007). English is mostly used by people in urban and semi-urban areas. There certainly is English in non-urban areas as well but not to the extent as in urban areas.

In the data of 1991 Census of India, 178,598 (87,896 male and 90,702 female) people across the country claimed English as their mother tongue ('Distribution of the Mother Tongues' 2007). Of these, 170,375 belong in urban areas and 8,223 in rural areas with a major concentration in Maharashtra of 84,448 English-speaking people.[1] As can be seen, the number of those who use English as a mother tongue (native language) is very small. However, the number of people who use English as

Figure 1.1 India 2006

a second language is considerably larger. According to the 1991 census, it stands at over 64 million (Satya 2007).

As of 2001, the literacy rate for the country is 64.8% (Registrar General and Census Commissioner, India 2007).[2] At about 28,000 books per annum, India is the third-largest publisher of English books in the world, after USA and UK (Shrivastava 2006). Taking Indian publication figures of 2004 into account, Satya (2007) states that, at around 23% of all titles published, the number of English publications is second only to Hindi. However, at twenty-three titles per 100,000 speakers, English is far ahead of Hindi in terms of the ratio of number of books published (five titles) in proportion to the number of English-language speakers.

As of 31 March 2006, there were 62,483 registered newspapers and periodicals, which included 2074 added during the year. The second largest in any given language is English with 9,064 newspapers and periodicals. Hindi tops the list with 24,927 publications ('Highlights' 2007).

The second and third largest circulating dailies are the English newspapers *The Hindu* with a circulation of 1,168,042 and *Hindustan Times* with 1,136,644. They are exceeded only by the Bengali daily, *Amrita Bazar Patrika* (1,234,122). The largest multi-edition daily is *The Times of India* (with a circulation of 2,542,075); and the largest circulated periodical is *The Hindu Weekly* (with 1,102,783) ('Highlights' 2007). According to 'Circulation pattern of English newspapers in India' (2007), the circulation of dailies, bi- and tri-weeklies grew from 8 million in 2000 to almost 11 million by 2005.

Further, given that only a minimum knowledge of English is required to navigate the Web or send an SMS, it is likely that the numbers of people with a functional knowledge of English will grow considerably, taking into consideration the penetration levels of both these media.

These facts show that, even if English is the native language of a miniscule minority, the number of people who can read and otherwise communicate in English is comparatively very large and growing.

1.3 Official status

This is how the official status of English is defined in the Constitution of India: English is an official language of the Union, by Article 343. It follows Hindi in this status. Article 343 grants this status for English for a period of fifteen years from the date of adoption of the Constitution, which happened in 1950.

At the approach of the fifteen-year deadline, the official language status of English was extended to an indefinite period of time, through the Official Languages Act, 1963. Designating English as an official language (along with Hindi) means that it is one of the languages used for all official purposes – that is, for government activities.

Further, the Constitution also states specifically the roles English will play in different contexts. States are to determine their official languages and also the languages to be used for inter-state communication and, in this, English is always an option open to the states. Some states, such as

Nagaland and Mizoram in the north-east, have designated English as their official language.

English does not figure among the eighteen languages of India listed in the Eighth Schedule of the Constitution. It figures as one of the ninety-six non-scheduled languages of the country. In Article 344 of the Indian Constitution, the role of English is indirectly defined. Future changes to language policy are to be determined by Commissions appointed by the President, who should bear in mind 'the industrial, cultural and scientific advancement of India, and the just claims and interests of persons belonging to the non-Hindi speaking areas' (*The Constitution of India*). Given the background of the period (see Chapter 5), this indicates that English should not be relegated to an unimportant position in deliberations regarding language policy. Thus, although the official language of India is first Hindi, English is given equal if not more importance. Incidentally, the Constitution itself was written originally in English and an authorised Hindi translation is now available.

1.4 Domains of use

The primary areas of English use are: education, administration, law, mass media, science and technology. English is the language of communication at the level of trade and commerce.

Again in Part XVII of the Constitution which defines the roles of the different languages, it is stated that all orders, rules and regulations and bye-laws etc., shall be in English. Moreover, the language of the High Courts and the Supreme Court is English. Quite apart from the official status accorded to English, here is an example of how English use has permeated some domains, almost irrevocably. The courts of justice require a certain type of knowledge, which is available only in English. Similarly, medicine, engineering, technology and all the sciences, which are all almost entirely taken from the West and its education systems, are in English. Indigenous systems were marginalised or wiped out during the colonial period and what survive now are probably available in small pockets. Ayurveda, which is a form of Indian medical science, is one such example. When knowledge and its dissemination are determined by Western standards, English must inevitably be used.

Among the educated classes, it is the first language used for communication. In everyday living, English plays a peculiar role. Even in the smallest of towns where English may be little known, the names of shops and other commercial establishments are often in English. This is true of very small establishments also. The use of two names is seen at the macro level as well. The Indian name for India is Bharat, common in Indian language usage; the country is defined in the Constitution as 'India, that is Bharat'.[3] The use of just a local language is rare for names of establishments though not unknown, especially in the Hindi-belt. Bhatia (1987) in a study of 1200 advertisements notes that about 90% of products had English names. Even when an Indian name is used, the tendency is to code-mix it with an English term: 'Morarji Fabrics', 'Vimal Suitings', 'Alok Industries'.

The role of English is therefore seen as that of a high language, used for certain specified purposes. Dasgupta (1993) argues that a diglossic situation prevails in India, where one variety of language ranks higher relative to the others, with English occupying the high position. In fact, he calls it 'the Auntie tongue' and emphasises that it is an 'other' language. At the level of the family and friends, English has restricted use. The topic being discussed is often a crucial determining factor for the language. Politics, education, medicine are likely to be discussed in English. Relationships and emotions are likely to be discussed in one's own language, especially by those who consider English to be a second language. Yet, personal letters are also written in English.

Overall, it is quite clear that English is not used in domains that are more emotional and non-intellectual. English is the language of the intellect and formality.

1.5 Cultural factors

Culture is a difficult term to define and even more difficult to identify, yet it touches all aspects of life – religion, social conduct, food, dress etc. An attempt is made here to delineate some of the influences of the English language on aspects of Indian culture, such as the performing arts and literature. This section only skims the surface of a vast topic.

It is not easy to determine those cultural aspects of Indian life that derive from English/Britain and those that derive from other Western countries. Western influence on India has existed since the fifteenth century. Britain was only one of the colonisers, albeit the most significant one. In modern times, American influence is also strong given the greater degree of migration to the United States and a constant movement of professionals between the two countries. In addition, generations of Indians have grown up on American fiction and Hollywood films. So, much of what is said in this section as the influence of English, must be juxtaposed with the distinct possibility of other European languages (besides English) and countries (other than Britain) having had inputs. In fact, with respect to overall lifestyle today, the influence of the

Portuguese on Goa is far greater and visible than the influence of the British on the rest of India.

Indian culture is rich in the arts – literature, music, dance, theatre, fine arts and, in modern India, cinema and television as well. But how much does English figure in all this?

Music is perhaps the most popular of all the arts and we find that classical Indian music continues its traditions. The two main types of music in India are the north Indian Hindustani and the south Indian Karnatic music. Both have deep traditions and changes only happen gradually. Concerts are usually by a vocalist or by a solo musician playing an instrument, with a minimum of percussionists. The vocalist or the soloist is the main persona and displays his/her calibre. The traditional Indian musical instruments are the veena, the sitar, the gottuvadyam, the sarangi, the sarod, the flute etc. Where outside influence is seen, it is in the use of Western instruments for Indian music, primarily in the use of the violin in Karnatic music which came to be an important instrument for concerts, both in a solo performance and as an accompanying instrument.[4] The smooth-flowing nature of the instrument was probably the main reason for its popularity. More recently, the mandolin has also been used for Karnatic music but this instrument does not have the same degree of popularity as the violin. The harmonium is used to set the pitch, especially by musicians in the north. But this Western instrument is considered to be unsuitable for Indian music and, in fact, All India Radio bans its use in its programmes ('South Asian arts' 2007).

Fusion music has been attempted by some musicians with some degree of success. The sitar maestro Ravi Shankar was among the first to attempt this with the Western musician Philip Glass. More recently, U. Srinivas, a mandolin player of Karnatic music, has brought out an album *Dream* with Michael Brook (Lal 2007). For the most part, this music is the result of collaboration. This type of music attempts to integrate elements of Indian classical with Western classical music. The degree of appeal of this type of music also rates below popular music and classical music.

Popular music came into its own with the advent of cinema. As Karnad (1995) puts it, at the end of the silent era, Indian films did not just talk but began to sing! Although other forms such as folk music exist, the most popular music for the common people in modern India is film music. Non-film bands exist for popular music but they are not as popular as film music. Music in Indian cinema brought about a novel innovation which is 'playback singing' using 'playback singers'. Quite apart from the new words, the concept is unique in that rarely do the actors in Indian films sing for themselves. Specialist singers perform this task.

It was in Indian film music that experimentation really began. In fact, Indian music was revolutionised as a result of cinema. Western music and Indian music were merged, both in harmony and the instruments that were used (Arnold 2000), and classical and folk elements were mixed. The concept of the orchestra took hold and the use of Western instruments modernised Indian music – the cello, the saxophone, the vibraphone, the mandolin etc., became part of the orchestra (Greene 2000). Many Western tunes, both classical and pop, have been either copied directly or have been adapted; an example is Jatin-Lalit's 'Chhad Zid Karna', in the film *Pyar Kiya to Darna Kya* (1998), which is a version of the British band Stereo Nation's song 'I've Been Waiting' (Arnold 2000).

Interestingly, however, the language of this music remains Indian – English is rarely used for songs in Indian films. An early exception is 'My Heart Is Beating', an English song in the Indian film *Julie* (1975). We find in the more recent *Lagaan* (2001), a Hindi song interspersed with English words. But this is primarily because the characters in these two films are an Anglo-Indian and a British woman respectively.

There are other instances of Indian songs being interspersed with English words. A notable example is in *Maro Charitra* (1978) in Telugu and its Hindi remake, *Ek Duuje ke liye* (1981). In these films, the two characters in love speak different Indian languages so, while the female voice sings in Telugu/Hindi, the male sings in English, the first words being 'I don't know what you say'. Towards the end of the Hindi-English song, the female singer translates what she is saying as 'We are made for each other', in English. A relatively recent film, *Criminal* (1995), has a song interspersed with English words, a rare example of a song in which English is not there for any specific reason. Kachru (2006) notes the use of English in Hindi film songs with examples, describing it as an aspect of code-switching. In her view, the use of English is primarily for fun and playfulness. Crucially, the point made by Kachru is that, even though, in general, English belongs to a high domain in India, in pop culture, it is like any other Indian language. Nevertheless, the point that English is not used seriously in music, even at the popular level, is still valid.

This does not mean that Indian English music is non-existent. There are bands, such as Indian Ocean, who sing in English but their popularity is limited and they definitely do not have the reach of popular Indian film music. Lou Hilt, a guitarist, traces the beginnings of Indian English music to Bengal (Pawar 2007). English bands began to sing even before Hindi bands came into existence in the 1970s. Initially they merely reproduced jazz music from the West. It was only gradually that they produced original music. He feels that the absence of good Indian

English music is primarily due to the poor pronunciation of otherwise good musicians. Those Indians who would like music in English have direct access to popular music from English-speaking countries. At the popular level, even among the English-educated, Indian English music has not yet made its mark.

Dasgupta (1993) notes the absence of Indian English in the arts. He cites the case of Indian music to show that the singers prefer to move to Hindi, the language with the maximum reach amongst Indian languages, citing the case of singer Sharon Prabhakar. He notes the absence of English in the other arts as well.

Modern Indian theatre is influenced by the London model, which came to India with the British in the late eighteenth century. Initially, theatre was meant for the entertainment of the British. Later, it became a source through which the local people were anglicised. British theatre introduced the proscenium stage among other things to Indians. As in all things modern, Bengal was the first to adopt the new form of theatre. In the mid nineteenth century, rich young Bengalis in Calcutta established theatres in their own homes and produced plays for their family and friends. These plays were based on British models and included song and music (see Sample 31, Chapter 7). With the success of these efforts, theatre was taken to the public arena. Theatre houses were established – Girish Chandra Ghosh founded the National Theatre in 1872 – and many features were taken from British models (Karnad 1995, 'South Asian arts' 2007). During the British Raj, theatre was primarily a source of articulating protest against the rulers which led to the Dramatic Performances Act 1879, which began censorship. To overcome this hurdle, Indian drama turned to history and mythology through which protest was expressed symbolically.

Theatre flourished in Bombay and Madras as well.[5] The languages used were Bengali in Calcutta, Tamil in Madras and, in Bombay, Marathi, Gujarati, Hindustani, Urdu and sometimes a combination of all these languages and English. Parsi theatre from Bombay, particularly, used European techniques, integrating them with local forms ('South Asian arts' 2007).

Indian English theatre begins with Utpal Dutt's Calcutta Little Theatre Group in 1947. Initially the plays performed by this group were in English; later, they changed to Bengali. Modern English playwrights whose plays have been performed are Girish Karnad, Manjula Padmanabhan, Mahesh Dattani and many others. The nineteenth-century phenomenon of music and song was dropped in favour of dialogue and realism in the twentieth century. The themes draw from a rich variety of sources, including Indian mythology and socially relevant topics. With the advent of cinema, theatre has gradually lost its audiences. Yet, it is not completely wiped out. Professional groups such as Prithvi Theatre in Bombay do exist and there are many amateur groups in India, some of which perform English plays, written by Western or Indian English writers. Amateur Indian English theatre exists primarily in colleges and universities where a college function is often marked by the performance of an English play.

Although Dasgupta claimed in 1993 that Indian English is not strong enough in the arts, it may not be incorrect to say that today films in Indian English are a seriously emerging genre. Yet, as in the case of television serials, the most popular films are in Indian languages; Bollywood (Hindi films made in Bombay/Mumbai) of course dominates the Indian film industry and is also a global cultural export. The Indian English films that are made in India (not to be confused with films made by non-resident Indians such as Mira Nair, Gurinder Chadha and others, whose audience is predominantly Western), are meant for the urban elite of India. The issues are such that the educated classes relate to them.

The first Indian film made by an Indian was *Raja Harischandra*, released in 1913. The first talkie was *Alam Ara* released in 1931. It was with the release of Aparna Sen's *36 Chowringhee Lane* in 1981 that Indian English films really caught the attention of the audiences. Recent films like *Mr and Mrs Iyer* (2002), *Jhankaar Beats* (2003) are meant for an English-speaking Indian audience and they also have the advantage of being accessible to audiences around the world. In these films, the characters use English and it is an essential part of their lives. Most of the characters are highly educated and have a westernised lifestyle. These films realistically portray a class of people in India for whom there is a social life of English (Sreetilak 2007). English in these films has a neutralising effect – that is, it enables a blurring of regional differences. Often, names reveal the background of the person. Yet, the advantage of English is that it gives the characters a secular and non-regional air. Most importantly, these films demonstrate the commonest feature of Indian life – use of English with strangers. When two strangers meet, the first language they use is English, until a common language is found. Often, even if they have a common language, unless a closer relationship is sought or established, use of English continues.

More recent Indian films use English as part of the dialogue without any apologies. This marks a change from earlier times when any use of English almost always meant an immediate translation of it into the language of the film. This was to enable comprehension by the audiences, the poorer sections in particular, for whom those films were primarily made. At the same time, the use of English was necessary to demonstrate that the character was well educated, upper class or insufferable. No such excuses are seen now. Films today no longer have the rich man versus poor man theme, with the necessary corollary that the rich man was evil and the poor one good. Wealth is taken for granted and so are foreign locales. Under such circumstances, use of English does not serve the specific purpose it did in earlier times. English is a necessary part of delineating the social background of the character. This is also because there is now a large expatriate Indian population in the West, which relates well to foreign lands and, of course, to English.

Using English names for Indian films in other languages is also common. For example, recent Telugu films have titles such as *Mass* (2004), *Boss* (2006) and so on. On the whole, English carries the same weight for naming that Sanskrit does. Most languages of India turn to Sanskrit to fill lexical gaps (in fact, there is explicit direction to this effect for Hindi in Article 351 of the Constitution of India). The Indian words for the government channels of television, Doordarshan, and radio, Aakaashvaani/All India Radio, for instance, are derived from Sanskrit. A similar role is played by English today at the common level. Also, interestingly, the most popular film magazines in India are in English – *Filmfare* and *Stardust*. These deal primarily with news from Bollywood, with a few sections for films from other languages.

Television is immensely popular in India, perhaps on a par with cinema. A distinction needs to be made between those channels that are based in the two major cities of India – Delhi and Bombay – and those in the rest of the country. Based in Delhi, Doordarshan is the official government channel. The Delhi- and Bombay- based private channels and foreign channels, such as Zee TV, Star TV, CNN-IBN, CNBC, NDTV etc., all conduct their programmes in Hindi and/or English. Other parts of the country have channels in local languages, including regional Doordarshan and regional channels. That is, at the national level, English and Hindi have primacy. However, the role of English is restricted to news programmes and to matters concerning political issues. Crucially, television serials are in Indian languages and very rarely in English, if at all. As with cinema, which deals with human emotions, it appears that television serials which touch the heart are also not acceptable to the audiences in a 'foreign' language. On the other hand, it is also a matter of economics. As seen above, the vast majority of Indians do not know English. The sheer numbers of the people who know Indian languages over English will obviously make films and television serials in Indian languages more popular.

Many talk shows are conducted in English; *We the People* and *The Big Fight* from NDTV often have the anchors changing languages from

English to Hindi, primarily to accommodate Hindi speakers who do not know English. Although there are other talk shows, *Koffee with Karan* is the first English show on Indian television to have the highest ratings in the country, with an estimated cumulative audience of 7.6 million (Pherwani 2005, Pillai 2005). The first season ran in 2004 and the second season in 2007. It is a weekly talk show that quizzes celebrities (mostly from Bollywood) on their lives and careers. As with the popular film magazines, celebrity life is mostly discussed in English. This, in turn, indicates that the urban elite who know English are just as interested in popular culture as the less-educated people for whom the films and television serials are purportedly made.

Whereas popularity is attained in the performing arts by using Indian languages, in the case of literature it is just the reverse. Indian English literature is the most developed of all the tangible English cultural phenomena and it has had a fair degree of growth in the twentieth century. In 1794, *The Travels of Dean Mahomet* was the first published work in English by an Indian (see Sample 1, Chapter 7). Yet the real beginnings lay in the poetry of the late nineteenth century, with writers using English imagery. This was perhaps to be expected, since the early writers such as the Dutt sisters, Toru and Aru, were educated in England and in Europe. Others were influenced deeply by English education and the writings of the English. Novelists of the early and mid twentieth century, such as R. K. Narayan, Mulk Raj Anand and Raja Rao, were conscious that they were writing in an alien language. Raja Rao states this as his predicament, in these oft-quoted lines (see also Sample 2, Chapter 7):

> One has to convey in a language that is not one's own, the spirit that is one's own. One has to convey the various shades and omissions of a certain thought-movement that looks maltreated in an alien language. I use the world 'alien', yet English is not really an alien language to Indians. It is the language of our intellectual make-up – like Sanskrit or Persian was before – but not of our emotional make-up. We are all instinctively bilingual, many of us writing in our own language and in English. We cannot write like the English. We should not. We cannot write only as Indians. We have grown to look at the large world as part of us. Our method of expression therefore has to be a dialect which will some day prove to be as distinctive and colourful as the Irish or the American. Time alone will justify it. (Rao 1974: v–vi)

Modern writers of literature no longer have this dilemma. English is as much their language, if not more, as the languages they are born to. As Kothari (2006) points out, there is actually a loss of the native language. Very often it is the native language that is not learnt, especially by those who constitute the diaspora or those who move across states within India. Even if such people manage to learn to speak 'their' language, they remain illiterate in it.

A recent issue of the magazine *The Week* ran a cover story, 'Emerging Indians' (2007), on the most promising young men and women from seven areas – politics, cinema, literature, entrepreneurship, sports, science and advertising. The winner in each category was selected by means of a survey which combined the inputs of an expert jury and voting. All the nominees in the category of literature were those who wrote in English and the category was classified as 'English Literature'. This marks the coming of age of what has been called, and in the academia continues to be called, 'Indian Writing in English'. What is crucial here is that, if the entire country is to be represented, it is done in English. But this is not so at the level of popular culture. In the category of cinema, all the nominees were from the Hindi film industry or were associated with it significantly. A related point is made by Kothari (2006) who points out that translating into English makes a translator in India. Translating into other languages is simply not on a par with translating into English.

1.6 'Indian English' versus 'English in India'

The term 'Indian English' is not one that all Indians are comfortable with. Over the years it has borne the connotation of 'bad English'. In the south of India, 'bad English' was called 'Butler English' (see Chapter 5). Parasher (1999b) traces this attitude back to British times. Krishnaswamy and Burde (1998) maintain very strongly that there is no such thing as Indian English. Their argument is based on written English which they claim is no different from standard English (British or American). They also give instances of so-called Indian English usages and draw parallels with American English. The use of Indian phonology and some lexical items does not make a distinct variety, according to them. They prefer to use the expression 'Indians' English'. Similarly, Dasgupta (1993) maintains that Indian English does not exist and that what we have are 'Indian Englishes'.

There are other scholars such as R. K. Agnihotri, Anju Sahgal, Aditi Mukherjee, Braj Kachru, Yamuna Kachru, S. N. Sridhar, Rakesh Bhatt for whom Indian English is an acceptable term. English is an Indian language for D'souza (2001) who does not agree with either Dasgupta's (1993) view of English as the 'other' or the modular approach of Krishnaswamy and Burde (1998). She provides a range of examples to demonstrate the penetration of English in a wide range of contexts.

In any case, the fact remains that, in India, those who consider their English to be good are outraged at being told that their English is Indian. Indians want to speak and use English like the British or, more lately, like the Americans. This desire probably also springs from the fact that it is a second language for most Indians and to be able to speak a non-native language like native speakers is a matter of pride – more so in the case of English, given its higher status and the several material advantages it carries.

In academia, as a result of this anathema towards 'Indian English', the preferred term has been 'English in India'. Another reason for this preference is also that 'Indian English' denotes linguistic features, whereas academics have been more interested in the historical, literary and cultural aspects of English in India.

It is important to note that there are no monolithic varieties of English in UK or USA. Davidson (2007) points this out and yet he says that there is a lot of similarity or homogeneity in the standard forms of English worldwide. India is no different. Just as there are varieties of British English, there are varieties of Indian English as well. The difference however lies in the fact that the different varieties of Indian English are not fixed in terms of their features, as will become apparent.

Other terms used are 'Inglish' (Hosali 1999), 'Indlish' (Sanyal 2006) and even 'interlanguage' (Tirumalesh 1990). Since it is a second language, it is believed that Indians can never reach the same competence as a native speaker. These terms imply overtly and implicitly that the Indian variety of English is substandard. However Kachru (1965, 1982) does make a distinction between the different types of IE that are used in India, ranging them on a cline of bilingualism that consists of three measuring points. The lowest ranked are the uneducated speakers who are at the zero point or the basilect – these include such people as guides, vendors and domestic staff. The central point or the mesolect consists of speakers who are less than well educated and generally are clerks, notaries etc. The ambilingual point or the acrolect is that of educated speakers such as civil servants, educationists, creative writers etc. The samples of the second variety are labelled Babu English (Sample 9, Chapter 7). Indian English as used by the third category of people is even equated with British standard English (for example, Sample 11, Chapter 7). Kachru's cline is also acknowledged by other scholars such as Lukmani (1992). The division among the varieties is not absolute and there is considerable overlap in this cline. That there is a standard variety of Indian English is accepted. This standard has been called educated Indian English and the circularity in giving this name has been acknowledged by both Parasher (1991) and Hosali (1999).

As Pattanayak says:

> The best reasons for calling English an Indian language may be said to be the feel of the educated Indian for the English language and the bidirectional pattern pressure exerted by the Indian languages including English on one another arising out of the density of communication involving these languages. (Pattanayak 1978: 187)

These lines emphasise the impact of Indian languages on English, which should be seen as an obvious corollary of the multilingual situation of English in India.

A discussion of Indian English almost invariably assumes that English is a second language for Indians and therefore high proficiency in English automatically implies that that the speakers are bilingual. Notice that the cline described above is called the cline of bilingualism and not one of proficiency in English. Bilingualism however is not essential. The figures of those who return English as their native language in the census is small but the number of Indians who would claim that English is their first language, even if they speak a different language at home, is very high. These speakers are not necessarily Anglo-Indians.[6] They are 'Anglophones' (Davidson 2007) – a more suitable term than the problematic 'native speakers'. Many creative writers who write in English fall into this category. Invariably, those educated people who grow up in a place where their language is not spoken end up with English as their first language.

In this book, 'Indian English' is used without apology because there is a variety of English that is identifiable as Indian; this variety has several different facets to it. There are Indian Englishes no doubt but they are Indian English first.

Notes

1. The 2001 Census of India has not yet released these figures.
2. Literacy figures are of those who are over seven years and can read and write. Those who can read but cannot write have been excluded from the list of literates in 2001 Census of India.
3. The name Bharat is not used in Tamil Nadu, the result of rejecting Sanskrit and Hindi. Intriguingly, Hindi movies always refer to India as Hindustan.
4. The violin is presumed to have been brought to India around 1790 by military bandmen of the East India Company, most of whom were Irish. It is also thought that Portuguese missionaries may have brought it with them for use in churches even earlier (Haigh n.d.).

5. Bombay is now called Mumbai, Madras is now Chennai and Calcutta is Kolkata, in an attempt to de-anglicise them. In this work, the earlier names are retained since these names were used during the period that we mostly cover.
6. The term Anglo-Indian originally referred to the British in colonial India. Now it refers to descendants of mixed marriages between Indians and Europeans.

2 Phonetics and Phonology

Indian English (IE) is best identified through its phonological features yet, paradoxically, the variation in the phonology is widespread. There is a standard variety of IE both in terms of phonology and syntax. It is essential, however, to maintain a distinction between the grammar and accent.

This chapter will deal with the standard accent and touch upon variation as well. Accent in Indian speech is marked by regional variation. Standard accent is usually devoid of regional markers but it is still identifiable as Indian by virtue of some pan-Indian features. There is also an intermediate accent that is more Indian than the standard, as a consequence of the extent to which the regional features appear in it.

Teachers of IE pronunciation have usually imposed an unattainable standard from the purely pedagogical point of view – Received Pronunciation (RP), which is the standard British accent from southern Britain. This has happened in spite of the fact that the British who came to India were from different parts of Britain. There were the Irish and Scots as well in colonial India. Many of the English themselves were not speakers of standard RP. Since English is taught as a second language in India, the issue of a standard for teaching has vexed and continues to vex classrooms. As early as 1800, an advertisement by William Carey from Serampore offering to teach English with particular attention to correct pronunciation appeared (Sinha 1978: 23–4).

Since a standard variety is usually taught in the second and foreign language classroom, RP has somehow become the standard of pronunciation to aspire to, at least from the point of view of educators. But, as stated earlier, this has never been achieved. True, there are schools, particularly convent schools that continue to place a great emphasis on correct pronunciation. In this process of attempting to acquire and impart RP, a variety of English has grown in the country that approximates RP yet has some distinctive features that mark it as Indian. This has de facto become the standard of pronunciation and is advocated by most educationists as the more appropriate norm for Indians. This variety has been labelled Educated Indian Pronunciation (Gokak 1964, Parasher 1991, Nihalani et al. 2005). CIEFL (1972) monograph on IE uses the term 'generalised IE' which is advocated for pedagogical purposes.[1] Chaudhary (1996) also addresses the issue of a teaching norm and suggests a globally usable and intelligible model rather than RP.

There are some differences in the descriptions in the texts mentioned above and the several others that deal with the Indian accent. An acquired variety modelled on RP is that of the newsreaders of All Indian Radio ('News on All India Radio' 2006). The variety that is described in this work, and one that is called the standard here, is close to but does not precisely match All India Radio newsreaders' speech. It is not the generalised IE that is mentioned above either. Generalised IE is the variety of speech that has more Indian features and is the second variety of the three types mentioned above.

Curiously, this standard cuts across the country and is usually free of regional features that mark the speech of most Indians. Whether the speaker is from Delhi, Calcutta, Bombay, Madras or Hyderabad, this is a speech variety that is Indian but of a higher status than other varieties. As can be seen, it is a variety belonging to urban places but this does not mean that all those who grow up in these places speak it or that others do not. Public schools and other elite schools, many of which are located in non-urban areas, seem to impart this variety.

In what follows, the features of this variety will be described. Since this is the variety that most Indians aspire to acquire, this variety will be considered to be the standard IE variety.[2] Those who speak the standard variety have a clear edge over those who do not and are more likely to get jobs; this is borne out very clearly in placement interviews on campuses. The vast majority of Indians do not speak this standard variety. Their accents tend to be regional in nature. The speech of Indians can be classified on the basis of the four geographical regions and further regions within them. Speech tends to be marked by elements from the native language or the most influential language in the repertoire of the speaker. Although the native language has some influence on accent, schooling and peer groups influence accent much more.

A cline of proficiency exists for IE as may be expected for a second language. This proficiency is at the level of grammar. Similarly, a cline of pronunciation exists that sets the standard variety at one end and the markedly regional varieties at the other end. The proficiency level in grammar and usage and the standard variety of pronunciation do not match in most cases. Fluent and proficient users of English often do not have a standard accent. In fact this is true of the vast majority of proficient users of English. The reverse – that of standard pronunciation but a lower level of proficiency in grammar and usage – is rare though not unheard of.

IE must be viewed more in terms of a set of features that may manifest themselves in the speech of individuals rather than as a constant. Individual variation is quite considerable in IE. The extent to which Indian features of pronunciation will occur in the speech of an individual varies from person to person. What follows therefore are, by and large, tendencies rather than absolutes.[3]

2.1 Consonant sounds

Consonants are described using three main criteria: place of articulation, that is, the point in the oral cavity where two organs come into contact with each other; manner of articulation, that is the way in which the air stream is closed and released; and voicing, that is whether the vocal cords vibrate or not.

2.1.1 /r/

Standard IE Pronunciation (SIEP) is non-rhotic, in which feature it matches RP. That is, the letter *r* in words like *card, park, smart, heart, bird, earth, purse*, where it occurs before consonant sounds, is not articulated. Also, it remains silent when it occurs in word-final positions as in *car, player, singer, sir* etc. Creative use of language is a part of advertisements and English is also used similarly. Non-rhoticity is made use of in this furniture advertisement, 'So fa, so good', and in this comment about the Congress President Sonia Gandhi, some years ago when she nearly became the Prime Minister, 'Sonia . . . and yet so far' (D'souza 2001: 153). An /r/-less accent is a prestige marker in India as Agnihotri and Sahgal (1985) and Sahgal and Agnihotri (1988) note.

Not pronouncing /r/ in the contexts specified above tends to be transferred to Indian names and words when one is speaking in English. *Uttar* ('north', 'reply') is an Indian (Hindi) word in which the final /r/ should be pronounced; still, it is not uncommon to hear *This is from Uttar Pradesh* where the /r/ is not pronounced as /uṭṭa pradeːʃ/, since the entire sentence is in English. Other examples of names are *Sharma* /ʃɜːmə/ instead of /ʃarmaː/ and *Verma* /ʋɜːmə/ instead of /ʋarmaː/. However, in AIR news Uttar Pradesh with /r/ pronounced, perhaps consciously, is usual. Thus, the phonology of IE tends to be maintained in units larger than the word and the same speaker would pronounce the same word differently in another language.

Accompanying this is the linking /r/, which surfaces in SIEP. That is, when words that end with the letter *r* are followed by words beginning with a vowel sound, the *r* is articulated as in: *The car* [r] *is here, The player* [r] *indicates his displeasure*. The final /r/ in the words *here* and *displeasure* in these two sentences is not pronounced.

The corresponding intrusive /r/, which is a feature of RP, is absent in IE. There is no /r/ articulation in phrases like *India and China, the idea of it*, which in RP may have a /r/ between *India* and *and* and between *idea* and *of*. Even the suggestion of such a pronunciation will seem ridiculous to Indians.

The influence of spelling on IE speech is quite well known. One early work is by Krishnamurti (1978). The absence of intrusive /r/ could be attributed to this fact. However, it is not possible to reduce all aspects of IE to spelling. The fact that SIEP is non-rhotic is proof of that.

Most non-standard varieties of IE are rhotic – that is, *r* is articulated in all the above contexts. There are those whose speech would be somewhere in the middle of the cline but they may still have non-rhotic speech.

There are several descriptions of the realisations of /r/ in IE. It has been called a post-alveolar frictionless continuant or an alveolar flap by Bansal (1976).

2.1.2 /v/ and /w/ or /ʋ/

Of the other distinctions that exist in RP, the difference between /v/ and /w/ is often absent in the speech of many IE speakers. But the distinction is maintained in SIEP. In articulating /v/, the front teeth touch the lower lip and the sound is a fricative, that is, air is released with audible friction. /w/ is articulated with rounded lips without contact. However, the amount of friction that /v/ carries in RP is greater than the friction in IE, even in the standard variety. The tendency however is to articulate another sound here without friction and, in fact, to replace it with the labio-dental approximant /ʋ/ which occurs in many Indian languages.

Non-standard varieties of IE do not maintain this spelling–pronunciation correspondence that prevails in English. Both /v/ and /w/ tend to be neutralised to the approximant mentioned above. Thus, the advertisement for a recent Hindi film that says 'villager, visionary, winner' is obviously meant to be alliterative. And the spelling error in a student answer script, 'They are playing wolly ball', is clearly due to just having heard the word and never having seen it in writing. The average Indian pronunciation does not provide clues as to the spelling, in this case.

2.1.3 /θ/ and /ð/ or /ṭ/, ṭh/, /ḍ/

It takes a lot of training and practice for Indians to master the fricatives /θ/ and /ð/ of English. The sound /θ/ is sometimes articulated in SIEP but /ð/ is almost completely missing. These dental fricatives are replaced by Indian dental plosives /ṭ/ or /ṭh/ and /ḍ/. The first sound in words like *through, thing, third* is the voiceless dental plosive. It is a sound for which the tongue touches the back of the teeth and cuts off air completely and the air is released suddenly. The dental sound is present in Indian languages and therefore it is easier in terms of articulation for speakers to replace the fricative. Since most of the words in which this sound is expected are written with *th*, aspiration of the plosive is heard. Indian languages barring Tamil have aspirated and unaspirated plosives. Usually, the aspirated version is heard in words like *things, thought* and *think*. This sound is determined by the spelling of the word; thus words like *Thames* and *Thomas*, which in native varieties of English have /t/ in the initial position, are articulated as /ṭh/ in IE.

The degree of aspiration is greater in the speech of those with an Indo-Aryan language background. And in the south, since Tamil does not have aspiration at all, Tamil speakers do not use /ṭh/. They systematically have /ṭ/ in the same words.

The voiced counterpart /ḍ/ of /ṭ/ is heard in words like *these, those, though* and others. That is, the difference between /ṭ/ and /ḍ/ lies only in the fact that the vocal cords vibrate in the articulation of the latter sound. In spite of the fact that Indian languages do have an aspirated voiced plosive /ḍh/, for some reason, this has not got transferred to their English.

2.1.4 /t/ and /d/ or /ṭ/ and /ḍ/

IE has been considered to be retroflex in the articulation of the first sounds in words like *today, tomorrow, terrific* and *demand*. That is, the tongue is said to curl backwards for these sounds and hit the hard palate. However, this is not universally correct. SIEP has alveolar sounds – that is, sounds in the articulation of which the tip of the tongue touches the alveolar ridge. The use of retroflexion is not necessarily uniform for the voiced and the voiceless sounds. While the voiceless /t/ is more frequent, it is the voiced /ḍ/ that betrays an Indian background. Khan (1989), in her study of variation among educated speakers of Aligarh, Uttar Pradesh, in north India, notes that there is variation in the speech of an individual depending on a number of factors including age, gender, social class, schooling and the context of the speech act. More formal situations bring on the alveolar sounds and the less formal bring on the retroflex sounds. Non-standard IE consistently uses the retroflex sounds.

2.1.5 The other consonants

Many of the consonants in IE match RP sounds. The other IE plosives are /p, b, k, g/. These symbols represent the initial sounds in the words *pin, bin, kin, gain* respectively. The affricates /tʃ, dʒ/ are also among the consonants of IE. These are sounds for which there is complete closure and slow release of air. Examples are the initial sounds in the following words *church, gin*. The fricatives are /f, s, z, ʃ, ʒ, h/. Examples for /f, s, z, ʃ, h/ are the initial sounds in the words *fin, sin, zebra, shy, hurry*. /ʒ/ is the initial sound in *genre* and the medial consonant in *measure*. All of these are prevalent in SIEP. Although CIEFL (1972) claims that /ʒ/ is problematic in generalised IE, it is definitely a consonant that exists in SIEP.

The nasal sounds are /m, n, ŋ/ in IE. These are perceived in the words *meet* (the initial sound), *neat* (the initial sound) and *sing* (the penultimate sound in IE, see 2.3.1). The lateral /l/ appears in IE as the initial sound in the words *luck, less*.

There are however, some regional variations which arise as a result of the features of the first languages of the speakers, which influence their English. So, some of the sounds described above tend to be replaced with local sounds close to them in articulation. All of these are non-standard. Some speakers with a Gujarati or Marathi background are likely to say /f/ as /ph/. For speakers with a Bengali, Oriya and Assamese background, /w, v/ are problematic because labio-dental sounds are in general difficult. They replace these sounds with /bh/. Bengali speakers also have a further problem distinguishing /s/ and /ʃ/. So do some Hindi speakers, from places like Bihar. These speakers tend to use either /s/ or /ʃ/ consistently in all contexts. /ʒ/ is unpronounceable for Kashmiris who replace it with /dʒ/. /h/ is generally unproblematic across the country. The letter *h* is pronounced as /hɛtʃ/. The nasal /n/ of other varieties is articulated as a retroflex sound by some South Indians. Thus *money* has /ɳ/.

As can be seen, it is not always that English sounds are replaced by regional equivalents. /ʒ/ is absent in Indian languages but has been acquired by most. On the other hand, /θ/ and /ð/ are also absent in Indian languages and are absent even in SIEP.

2.1.6 Non-contrastive sounds

Aspiration is contrastive in Indian languages, barring Tamil. So, /pal/ 'moment' is different from /phal/ 'fruit' in Hindi. This makes /p/ and

/ph/ contrastive sounds or phonemes. On the other hand, in RP, aspiration occurs in specific contexts. Since the context is determined, it becomes obligatory. [ph, th, kh] are the only aspirated sounds in English. And these occur in the initial position of stressed syllables. Thus [p] in *pin, upon, suppose* is aspirated, whereas [p] in *spin, capers* is not aspirated. This makes [p] and [ph] non-contrastive in English. That is, even if one did not (deliberately) aspirate /p/ in words like *pin, upon*, the words would not be considered to be different words. They are still the same word.

In IE, aspiration does not work the way it does in RP. It is non-contrastive but not entirely predictable. Where aspiration does occur, it is the result of spelling. But, as seen above, spelling does not induce aspiration of /d̪/. This is not a difference between voiced and voiceless sounds either because /g/, which is a voiced sound, does show aspiration. Thus, *ghost* and *ghastly* have an initial aspirated sound [gh]. In some words like *John*, even though the *h* is not immediately after *j*, aspiration is heard as [dʒh]. Influence of spelling is nevertheless seen when *h* occurs in the spelling. The tendency is to make the sound an aspirated sound. In SIEP sometimes words with *wh-* are aspirated – *why* /vhai/ or /whai/.

Again, spelling influences the articulation of the first sound in words like *change, challenge*, which tend to be aspirated. Wiltshire and Harnsberger (2006) note an interesting point in their data about aspiration in Tamil English. It is in this variety that aspiration is heard in the initial plosives, precisely because it is non-contrastive. Yet, the voicing contrast which is also absent in Tamil is acquired by Tamil speakers of English and sounds like /p/ and /b/ are not confused.

Another non-contrastive distinction known in RP is the difference between [l] and [ɫ], known as clear l and dark l respectively. Clear l occurs in most contexts but dark l occurs when it is followed by a consonant or by a pause in words such as *milk, bulb, feel*. Dark l is completely absent in IE, including the standard variety and clear l is used in all contexts.

In non-standard IE, what might appear is the retroflex /ɭ/ in south Indian speech in words like *colour, play*. The deeper south one goes, the greater the degree of retroflexion of /ɭ/. Retroflex /ɭ/ is absent in SIEP. Again although, /l/ and /ɭ/ are contrastive in Indian (Dravidian) languages, they are not contrastive in IE. Similarly, /n/ and /ɳ/ are contrastive in most Indian languages, yet they are not contrastive in IE.

Further, Tamil and Malayalam have a rule of voicing a plosive when it is between vowels or when it follows a nasal. This phenomenon tends to be transferred to the English speech of such speakers. A restaurant that had a special food festival attracted customers with the advertisement 'Simbly [sɪmbɭɪ] South' in which 'simbly' is meant to be 'simply'.

In Dravidian languages, /j/ and /w/ are optional in the word-initial position. Their occurrence is determined by the quality of the initial vowel that occurs in the word. Thus, if a word begins with a front vowel (see 2.2 on vowels), /j/ can be inserted optionally – /idi/ and /jidi/, 'this', are the same word in Telugu. Similarly, if the first vowel is a back vowel, /w/ is optional – /okaṭi/ and /wokaṭi/, 'one', are synonymous and are the same word. In the speech of many Dravidians, this phenomenon is transferred to English. Thus, *only* becomes /wonlɪ/ and it is perfectly normal to hear /jes/ for *s* and /es/ for *yes*, and *yearned leave* for *earned leave*. SIEP does not carry this feature.

Thus the consonants of SIEP are:

1.

Plosives:	p, b, t/ṭ, d/ḍ, t̪/t̪h, ḍ, k, g
Fricatives:	f, v, s, z, ʃ, ʒ, h
Affricates:	tʃ, dʒ
Nasals:	m, n, ŋ
Lateral:	l
Approximants:	ʋ, r
Semi-vowels:	j, w

2.2 Vowel sounds

Vowels are described based on three main criteria: the part of the tongue that is used in articulation (which is described as front, central or back); the height to which it is raised (high or close, half-close, half-open and low or open); and the degree of lip rounding. Vowels are of two kinds – pure vowels and diphthongs. Pure vowels are either long or short. These vowels have only one quality throughout the articulation. Diphthongs are vowel sounds that glide from one quality to another. There are usually two identifiable sounds in a diphthong.

2.2.1 The short vowels

The short vowels in SIEP are more or less the same as those in RP, with one exception. The distinction that exists between the truly central vowel /ə/ and the lower central vowel /ʌ/ is sometimes neutralised in SIEP or the two vowels are used as free variants (Bansal 1978).

PHONETICS AND PHONOLOGY 25

The short vowels in IE are thus /ɪ, ɛ, æ, ɒ, ʊ, ʌ, ə/, although the last two may be neutralised. Examples of words in which short vowels occur are: /ɪ/, the first vowel in the words *sit, bitter, skin*; /ɛ/, *red, better*; /æ/, *cat, battle*; /ɒ/, *hot, cot*; /ʊ/, *put, pull*; /ʌ/, *butter, putty*; /ə/, *appear, allow*.

In non-standard varieties, the two sounds /ʌ/ and /ə/ are neutralised. Sometimes, another sound /a/ which is more open than the English central sound is heard in place of /ʌ/.

In non-standard English pronunciation, /ɒ/ is not articulated; in its place, the vowel used is usually /a/, so *hot* is /hat/. This is particularly true of south Indian Tamil, Kannada and Telugu speech. Malayalam speakers tend to use a long or a short /o/ in words like *John*, which can approximate *Joan*.

2.2.2 The long vowels

The long vowels are /iː, eː, aː, ɒː, oː, uː, ɜː/. While RP has five long vowels, SIEP has seven. Words that have /iː/ are *seat, beat*; /aː/ appears in *card, master*; /uː/ is heard in *boot, pool*.

The most important difference between RP and SIEP lies in the long vowels /eː/ and /oː/. These do not exist in RP which has diphthongs instead. These diphthongs are rarely articulated in SIEP. /eː/ is heard in words like *day, may, play*. And /oː/ is heard in words like *no, go, groan*. In some contexts, generally in word-final positions as in *today*, these vowels are shortened to /e/ and /o/ respectively. There is a qualitative difference between the short /ɛ/ and the shortened /e/. The former is a bit lower in articulation. Similarly, there is a qualitative difference between short /ɪ, ʊ/ and the long /iː, uː/. The short vowels are a little lower and more central than the long vowels.

The other difference lies in the quality of the back vowel in words like *bought, daughter* which are /bɒːt/ and /dɒːtə/ respectively. While the RP sound is higher, the Indian sound tends to be merely a longer version of /ɒ/. Only those who are specially trained articulate /ɔː/ and this sound is sometimes heard in the speech of All India Radio newsreaders. In non-standard accents, the equivalent is /aː/.

The long vowel /ɜː/ occurs in words like *bird, curd, dearth*. It appears in SIEP which is non-rhotic. When the accent is rhotic, the words are articulated as /bard, kard, darṯ/ or /bərd, kərd, dərṯ/.

2.2.3 Diphthongs

There are six diphthongs in SIEP. Thus we have /ɪə/ as in *here, peer, beer*; /ʊə/ as in *poor, tour, cure*; /eə/ as in *fair, pair, hare*; /aɪ/ as in *night, right*, *gripe*, /ɒɪ/ as in *boil, toy, coin*; and /aʊ/ as in *cow, town, growl*. It is in non-standard IE that variation from these sounds is heard. The tendency in non-standard IE is to convert diphthongs other than /aɪ/ and /aʊ/ to long vowels as *beer* /biːr/, *poor* /puːr/, *tour* /tuːr/, *fair, fare* /feːr/, *pear* /peːr/. Those who do not articulate /ɒ/ and /ɒː/ do not do so in the diphthongs either. Thus *boil* is /baːɪl/ and coin is /kaːɪn/.

The vowels of IE are as follows:

2.

Short vowels:	/ɪ, ɛ, æ, ʌ, ə, ɒ, ʊ/
Long vowels:	/iː, eː, 3ː, aː, ɒː, oː, uː/
Diphthongs:	/aɪ, ɒɪ, aʊ, ɪə, ʊə, eə/

2.3 Other aspects of segments

2.3.1 Spelling pronunciation

The influence of spelling is apparent in the pronunciation of certain sounds as we saw above. Some further patterns can also be observed. In words that have *ng* in the spelling, both letters are articulated irrespective of the position in the word: *finger* /fɪŋgə/, *sing* /sɪŋg/, *singer* /sɪŋgə/, *singing* /sɪŋgɪŋg/ etc. In this respect, SIEP is different from RP – in the latter, only /ŋ/ is articulated word finally but not /g/ as /sɪŋ/. Words that are derived from these such as *singer* and *singing* also have a silent *g* in RP. Very few SIEP speakers are likely to have the kind of articulation that RP has. Words like *climb* and *dumb* also have the final /b/ articulated. /b/ is articulated in *plumber* and *plumbing*.

Another strong influence of spelling is seen in geminate articulation of consonants. In words such as *summer* /sʌmmə/, *happy* /hæppɪ/, *killing* /kɪllɪŋg/, *bitter* /bɪttə/ or /bɪtt̪ə/, double articulation of the medial consonants is evident. This is also true of words that have two separate letters that could stand for the same sound such as *lucky*. Krishnamurti (1978) maintains that this double articulation is evident only where there is a short vowel on either side in disyllabic words. If a long vowel precedes the double consonant, then it is not articulated as a double consonant due to a pan-Indian length alternation rule between vowels and consonants. One may say that in words like *usually, questionnaire, beginning, command* double articulation of *ll, nn* and *mm* is absent either because the word is not disyllabic or because the preceding or following vowel is long. All the words barring *command* are polysyllabic. The word *command* although disyllabic, has a long vowel /a:/ after *mm*. Hence it does not show geminate articulation. Moreover, when there is a prefix in the word, invariably there is double articulation – *unnatural* /nn/, *irresponsible* /rr/, *illegal* /ll/, *immobile* /mm/ and so on. In words like *immensely* double articulation is heard. Further, emphasis and exaggeration bring on double articulation – in *You will be utterly miserable*, *utterly* can have /tt/ in emphatic speech.

Other influences are seen in words such as *judge* in which all the consonants may be articulated as /dʒədhʒ/ and *edgy* would be /edhʒɪ/.

Another aspect related to spelling also prevails. Since a number of English words are merely heard (often mispronounced) and are not seen in printed form by a multitude of Indians, it is not uncommon to see misspellings in signs across the country. Some examples are *will* for *wheel*, *rasberry* for *raspberry* etc. This is true of educated Indians as well; students have such spellings as *wholistic*, *vocal chords*, *auxillary* etc.

2.3.2 Some specific words

Unlike with consonants, spelling is often no indicator of the quality of vowel to be used. Length can be a problem – *truth* is articulated by some as /trut̪/ and *stove* is either /stoːʊ/ or /staʊ/ depending on the speaker. The latter is more of a non-standard pronunciation. In non-standard pronunciation, *mundane* is /mʊndeːn/, *nasty* /næstɪ/ etc. Thus, *pears* is articulated as /pɪərs/, *prefer* as /prefə/.

At times though, spelling seems to have a deep influence as in the word *performance* which is /perfaːrmens/ in the speech of some speakers. When the pronunciation is rhotic, very often the preceding vowel is short – *purpose* is /parpəs/, *surplus* is /sarpləs/.

In the pronunciation of individual words one does not see an exact replacement of the Indian vowel for the RP vowel; thus *bored* is /boːd/, not /bɒːd/, *store* is usually /stoː/ and *four* usually /foː/. And, *cot*, *caught*, *court* are distinguished like this – /kɒt/, /kɒːt/ and /koːt/. The words *spot* and *sport* are /spɒt/ and /spoːt/ respectively. In non-standard IE varieties, *r* is articulated – /boːrd/. The distinction between words that sometimes occurs in RP is lost in all varieties of IE – *mourn* and *moan* are both pronounced as /moːn/.

Sometimes, even if the spelling is an indicator, some pronunciations are established, probably due to analogy – *food* is /fʊd/, like *wood* /ʊʊd/ in non-standard IE, and *soot* is /suːt/ in SIEP.

A semi-vowel is often inserted in words like *India* /ɪndɪjə/ and *our* /ʌwə/. Some examples of IE pronunciation of some words are given below:

3.

serious	/siːrɪəs/
furious	/fjuːrɪəs/
hero	/hiːroː/
zero	/ziːroː/

2.3.3 Morphophonology

There is a great deal of predictability in the way in which suffixes are articulated. The plural suffix is invariably /s/ or /ɛs/ in speech:

4.

cats	/kæts/
dogs	/dɒgs/
keys	/kiːs/
trains	/treːns/
horses	/hɒːsɛs/

The plural marker is realised in RP as [əz] or [ɪz] when the final consonant of the word to which it attaches is one of the following: / tʃ, dʒ, s, z, ʃ, ʒ/. In IE, however, it is [ɛs] in these contexts. Sometimes it could be [ɛz]. Occasionally, one might hear [əz]. Also, when voiced consonants other than those in the above list occur word finally, the plural is often realised as [s] in IE and occasionally as [z].

Similarly, the past tense marker is always /d/ or /ɛd/ depending on the word to which it attaches:

5.

played	/pleːd/
trapped	/træpd/
trained	/treːnd/
climbed	/klaɪmbd/
posted	/poːstɛd/

In this respect, IE is different from RP which has [əd] or [ɪd] when the final consonant is /t/ or /d/. And, when the final consonant is a voiceless sound other than /t/, in RP the past tense marker is realised as [t]. In IE, when the final consonant is /t/ or /d/, the past tense marker is [ɛd]. Occasionally [əd] is used. And in all other contexts, /d/ is used.

Other suffixes have full vowels:

6.

| hopeless | /hoːplɛs/ |
| happiness | /hæpɪnɛs/ |

2.3.4 Simplification of consonant clusters

Consonant clusters tend to be problematic for many Indian speakers. There are several different ways in which the clusters are simplified across the country. The commonest way is to delete some consonants. For instance, a word like *texts* is pronounced as /tɛks/. Similarly *acts* tends to be /æks/. This is seen in SIEP as well. Khan (1991) in her study of one variety of IE (Uttar Pradesh, north India) shows that /t/ or /d/ in a word-final cluster is deleted when it is followed in a sentence by a consonant. So the final consonants in words like *fast, missed* are deleted particularly when followed by other consonants.

In SIEP and non-standard varieties, there are no syllabic consonants in words like *castle, bottle, cycle, button, cotton*. A vowel /ə/ or /ɪ/ is inserted before the last consonant. However, in SIEP word-final cluster *lm* is not a problem in words like *film*. In non-standard IE it is usually /fɪləm/.

Most of the other ways of simplifying consonant clusters are features of non-standard varieties. Words like *station* become /ʈeːsən/. This word in particular has been assimilated into south Indian languages and this is the pronunciation in local languages. In the Hindi-Punjabi areas, a vowel is inserted either before or within the consonant cluster: *school* is /ɪskuːl/ or /səkuːl/.

2.4 Suprasegmental features

2.4.1 Stress

Just as there is unpredictability in the pronunciation of individual words and segments, stress, which is the relative prominence with which a syllable is uttered, also tends to be unpredictable. By and large, in SIEP, it may not be incorrect to say that each word is learnt separately for its stress. If words such as *exami'nation, con'dition* have stress on the penultimate syllable, the logic is not carried to *a'bolition* and *pre'monition* in which words the Indian tendency is to stress the ante-penultimate syllable.

There are several works on IE stress focussing on specific regional varieties of IE, such as Vijayakrishnan (1978), Sethi (1980), Sadanandan (1981), Shuja (1995), Das (2001) and so on. But all these works focus on only one aspect or one region. Moreover, several of these works admit that there is a great deal of variation even within a variety, so much so that generalisation is often difficult.

Chaudhary (1989) is among the works that attempt to give a pan-Indian account of stress in IE. More recently, Gargesh (2004) also has given some principles for IE stress and Wiltshire and Moon (2003) have attempted to identify the acoustic correlates of stress in IE. One factor that emerges from most of these works is that stress placement in IE is dependent on the weight of the syllable. That is, a syllable is said to be light if it contains just one short vowel. The number of consonants that precede the vowel is immaterial to the weight of the syllable – CV is the form taken by a light syllable. A heavy syllable is one in which there is a long vowel or a vowel along with a consonant – V: or VC. An extra heavy syllable is one in which there is either a long vowel followed by at least one consonant or a short vowel followed by at least two consonants – V:C or VCC.

A simplified version of the rules given by Gargesh (2004) is as follows: stress falls on the first syllable of a bisyllabic word unless the second syllable is extra heavy. Thus the stress in the following words is explained: 'taboo, 'mistake, 'monsoon, 'concrete. In trisyllabic words, the stress is also on the first syllable unless the second syllable is heavy, in which case the second syllable takes the stress. Thus the following stress pattern emerges: mo'desty, cha'racter, mi'nister, 'terrific and so on. Gargesh's rules do not account for several variations that prevail in IE. These rules cannot explain why some Indians have the following stresses in the same words: ta'boo, mis'take, 'modesty, 'character, 'minister, ter'rific.

The second factor that emerges particularly from Chaudhary's (1989) work is that there are differences in stress placement between the Indian Englishes of the Indo-Aryan group of speakers and the Dravidian group of speakers. These differences are somewhat systematic. Syllable weight plays an equally important role in both language groups. However, the manner in which a word is syllabified varies between the two groups. Thus syllabification makes a difference to stress placement. The different syllable structures assigned take care of the initial stress in 'minister of Dravidian speakers who would syllabify the word as mi.ni.ster whereas the Indo-Aryan group perceives it as mi.nis.ter. Chaudhary's is a more comprehensive account of word stress in IE.

However, it still leaves some questions. For instance, there is no apparent explanation for why some speakers stress the second syllable in *de'velop, con'sider, e'licit* and so on.

The variation in stress in the speech of an individual or within a group may perhaps be ascribed to the following – the default stress pattern of IE speakers is the kind described by Chaudhary (1989), which is based on their specific language background. When confronted with a new word, speakers of IE fall back on the stress pattern of their native languages. When their speech deviates from their own patterns and conforms to RP, it is the result of being taught the words separately or of having acquired a different stress pattern from their sources, which could very well be Indian. Prabhakar Babu (1971a, 1971b) notes in a small experiment that there is about seventy percent agreement in the stress patterns of the words between IE and RP.

So, if a Dravidian speaker pronounces *de'velop* with stress on the second syllable, it is a specially acquired characteristic. Chaudhary (1989) in fact takes the view that some features of the native phonology of English have been retained in IE. Most speakers of SIEP make an effort to acquire the stress patterns of RP or these are entrenched sufficiently in their education system for them to have acquired them unconsciously. In nonstandard IE, however, these special patterns are absent and the speech is true to the stress patterns of their own language. What remains to be seen is the extent to which conformity to RP stress patterns may be attributed to natural stress patterns of the speakers' native language and to special acquisition. It may be almost impossible to establish this unless developmental studies of children are undertaken.

As a direct consequence of the general tendency, abbreviations are stressed on the first syllable even in SIEP, not the last as in native varieties. There are no inputs in India with stress on the last syllable in these cases.

7.
IE	native Englishes
'TV	T'V
'BBC	BB'C
'ECG	EC'G

Similarly, compound stress is also on the first item rather than the second in all cases:

8.
'loud speaker
'bad-tempered

'headquarters
'three-wheeler
'typewriter
'car-ferry

(words from Roach 2000: 235)

The distinction in stress that exists in RP between noun or adjective on the one hand and verb on the other in some words is often absent in IE.

9.
N/A	V
'insult	in'sult
'abstract	abs'tract
'import	im'port
'conduct	con'duct

It may exist sporadically in some sets of words in SIEP but usually the grammatical difference is not brought out by stress in non-standard IE. Thus the IE forms tend to be consistent as below:

10.
N/A/V
'insult
'abstract
'import
'conduct

Again the tendency is to stress the first syllable but an occasional word like *con'duct*, when used as a verb, may be stressed on the second syllable. Words with *-teen* are stressed on the first syllable in IE:

11.
'thirteen
'fifteen
'seventeen

If word stress is unpredictable, sentence stress is even more so. In contrast to RP, IE tends to have stress on many words in a sentence. A sentence like *Ramesh will come late to the party as usual* tends to have stress on all the content words.

There is a tendency in IE to stress the initial pronoun in the following sentences:

12.

(a) 'He is saying that two is too much.

(b) 'She took leave for two years.

(c) 'They asked for it.

News channels have speakers who stress words like *will* which is very different from RP in which, unless there is a contrast being indicated, *will* will not be stressed. So, *The Prime Minister* '*will fly to Moscow tomorrow* is often said with stress on *will* even though it is a purely routine piece of information.

Stewart (2003) observes that a trend of stressing unimportant words is emerging in American English. He notes this of newsreaders of American radio and television channels who say *This* '*is the CBC*. Also, breaking up of sentences in unexpected places conveys the wrong or ambiguous meaning. He suggests that this trend is spreading to British English and also to speech not of the media. One of his arguments is that this may be due to the fact that newsreaders do not have the entire script in front of them and read fragments at a time so, to be safe, stress more words than necessary. IE has always been this way and there is no evidence to claim that this is the result of modern influence on modern IE. This may be true of Indian media but the speech of Indians has tended towards stressing unimportant words and pausing between unrelated phrases.

The difference between content words (those that carry the main meaning in a sentence) and function words (those that are important for the grammaticality of a sentence) is not maintained in pronunciation in IE. SIEP is close to RP with regard to stress in sentences to the extent that content words and words with emphasis or contrast are stressed.

The crucial difference between RP and IE lies in the relatively fewer weak forms in the latter. That is, function words between stressed content words tend to be reduced in articulation in RP. This is the result of the rhythm of RP. Since IE does not have the same rhythm as RP, the reduction apparent in RP is not seen to the same degree in IE, including SIEP. For example, *of* is fully articulated in such sentences as *I am afraid of death*. Moreover, the /v/ seen in RP is again absent in IE – it is always /ɒf/. However, it is not as if weak forms are always absent. The word *and* is often reduced to /ən/. The phrase *bread and butter* has a reduced *and*.

2.4.2 Rhythm and intonation

Rhythm in native varieties of English is said to be stress-timed, which means that the time taken to move from one stressed syllable in a sentence to the next is approximately the same. This is irrespective of the number of intervening syllables. IE rhythm has been said to be derived from the rhythm of Indian languages which is supposed to be syllable-timed – that is, the time taken to utter each syllable is the same.

The statement often made that IE stress is syllable-timed (for instance, by Gargesh 2004) is not verified completely. As Roach (2000: 138) points out, the difference between stress-timed and syllable-timed languages is not so clear. The implication of syllable-timed rhythm suggested for IE is that there are no weak syllables or weak forms, which is certainly not the case. There is in fact a case for maintaining that IE rhythm is not syllable-timed. Prabhakar Babu (1971a, 1971b), in an experiment done to establish this, found that IE rhythm is neither stress-timed nor syllable-timed. Considering the manner in which stress operates in IE, which is sensitive to the weight of the syllable, and the observation that length is a correlate of stress, syllable-timed rhythm is a matter for research in IE. Further, the existence of weak forms in connected speech demonstrates quite clearly that IE rhythm cannot be syllable-timed.

In the example given by Gargesh (2004) of the sentence 'I am thinking of you', it is claimed that all the words are stressed and therefore each syllable gets prominence. However, SIEP users will definitely reduce *I am* to *I'm*.

Although very little work has been done on IE intonation, some facts are clear. When asked to judge the meaning(s) conveyed by sentences that carry the falling intonation, the rising intonation and the fall-rise, hearers uniformly identify the following meanings: the falling intonation indicates statements; the rising intonation indicates questions; and the fall-rise indicates incompleteness or reservation.

In general in IE, greater use of the falling and the rising intonation patterns is seen. Normal statements are said with a falling intonation.

13.

   (a) This is my ↘book

   or

   (b) This is ↘my book.

14. This is very ↘funny.

As noted earlier there is a tendency to stress pronouns. And, even if there is no particular contrast involved, the likelihood of *my* being stressed and thereby taking the falling tune is high.

Most *wh*-questions are said with a falling intonation. Culturally, India is quite hierarchy minded and also generally polite to strangers. Therefore, with subordinates, the use of the falling intonation is common and, with newcomers, the use of the rising intonation. *Wh*-questions, when put to strangers, have a rising intonation.

15.

(a) What's your ↑name?

(b) Where do you ↑live?

The same questions put to one's social inferiors will have a falling intonation. Teachers would put the same questions to students as:

16.

(a) What's your ↓name?

(b) Where do you ↓live?

Yes-no questions are said with a rise and so are statements that are used as questions:

17.

(a) Are you ↑Nirmala?

(b) You are ↑waiting?

Non-standard pronunciation uses these patterns rather differently. Many announcements, especially at airports and railway stations tend to end with a rise, often giving the hearer a sense that something more is coming. Such statements as the following end with a rise.

18. The train will arrive on platform number ↑four.

Shuja (1995) notes for Urdu-English that the use of the falling, rising and the falling-rising tunes are more common than other more complex tunes. This is true of most varieties of IE. One hears the falling tone most of all and then the rising tone. This is borne out in the intonation of the informants in Prabhakar Babu's (1971a) experiment as well. There are more falling and rising tunes than the fall-rise.

Wiltshire and Harnsberger (2006) note that there is considerable difference in the use of pitch-accent between two groups of speakers – Tamil speakers (belonging to the Dravidian language family) and Gujarati speakers (belonging to the Indo-Aryan language family). The preference of the Tamil speakers is to use a fall and that of the Gujarati speakers is to use a rise. There is an overall tendency to use pitch changes on several words in an utterance also.

IE prosody is further complicated by the fact that pauses do not always occur at sense groups. They tend to occur rather randomly. Such pauses as indicated below are common:

> 19. Train number// 2734 from Secunderabad to// Tirupati will arrive on// platform number one.

Or a recorded message of a telephone service is likely to be:

> 20. The phone you are trying to reach// is busy. Please// try again later.

As a result of such pauses for which generalisations are difficult, the intonation pattern or pitch change is also difficult to establish. This aspect of IE requires further investigation.

2.4.3 Other aspects of connected speech

Some phonological features of connected speech in IE are that emphasis, exaggeration and surprise are expressed through lengthening – both of consonants and vowels. Retroflex tends to become prominent when one is emotional.

> 21.
> - (a) I had so much fun. [extra long /o:/ in *so*]
> - (b) Series of stories. [extra long /i:/ in *series*]
> - (c) Great poetry. [extra long /e:/ in *great*]
> - (d) It was the happiest day of my life. [extra long /p/ in *happiest*]
> - (e) It was killing. [extra long /l/ in *killing*]

These are all quite common in non-standard speech and are sometimes heard in SIEP as well.

SIEP has the /ə/ /ɪ/ distinction before consonants and vowels with the:

22.

(a) His is the [ɖə] best work.

(b) The [ɖɪ] easy-chair is comfortable.

This distinction may not always apply in non-standard IE. It tends to be universally /ɖɪ/ or /ɖə/ depending on the speaker.

2.5 Variation in individual speakers

As stated at the outset, a standard accent in an individual is not a constant or a perfect set of all the sounds identified as standard. An /r/-less accent may be accompanied by a retroflex plosive in the speech of an individual. That is, a feature or two that are identified as non-standard may occur in otherwise standard speech. The most important feature that seems to mark a standard accent is an /r/-less accent. A rhotic Indian accent is not a standard accent.

That IE must be placed on a cline by way of accents is explicitly or implicitly stated in many works. Notable in this regard are the works of Agnihotri and Sahgal (1985) and Sahgal and Agnihotri (1988), who organise their informants into three groups based on the type of education and schools attended. The more elite schools evidently impart an elite accent consciously. In addition to a general accent that an individual has, the context also can change the accent. Thus what are identified as non-standard above would surface in the speech of a speaker of SIEP if the situation is one of informality or if the other interlocutor speaks a non-standard variety. A non-rhotic accent can and does become a rhotic accent if one is talking to a shopkeeper whose accent is non-standard and rhotic. So also with retroflexion and other vowel sounds. Taking a few features of IE, Sahgal and Agnihotri (1988) examine the variation that exists according to the style of speech – reading and casual. The use of retroflex sounds and /r/ articulation increases in the casual speech of speakers.

These studies emphasise the social dimension of IE accents. The complexity of IE pronunciation is such that one account simply cannot take care of all the varieties that exist, as is the case for the English speech of any country.

In the preceding sections, we noted that there are regional variations. However, an aspect that warrants further investigation is the hypothesis proposed by Thundy (1976) that the IE accent is the result of various influences from Britain. He draws parallels between some IE segmental features and the features of different British accents. Many of the first speakers and teachers of English in India, as stated earlier, were not those who spoke RP but were from different strata and from across the British Isles. Therefore, some of the features of IE listed above may be remnants of those British accents to which Indians once had access.

Notes

1. The audio cassettes produced by the Central Institute of English and Foreign Languages (CIEFL) (now called the English and Foreign Languages University) which are used for teaching purposes are modelled on RP.
2. Although classes on pronunciation are derided, most classes and courses on pronunciation are well attended, even if they are not too successful. Language learning theories do show that changing one's accent in adulthood is difficult.
3. As Wiltshire (2005) rightly points out, most of the work on IE has focused on speakers with language backgrounds that are either Indo-Aryan or Dravidian. Hers is a descriptive account of the English of speakers with a Tibeto-Burman language background. These features appear to be different from the varieties of IE we are considering.

3 Morphosyntax

The syntax of Indian English, as opposed to phonology and lexis, is said to conform most to standard British English. There are some who believe that Indian English tends to be stylistically different from Western standards, even if it is syntactically close to standard British or American English. It is considered to be more formal, with a preference for certain syntactic forms. Debate marks this issue. As in the case of the phonology of Indian English, syntax too may be placed on a cline – this time of proficiency. The more proficient speakers, with exposure to Western standards, tend to use a form of the grammar that is very close to standard British English (BE) or American English (AE). The less proficient have features that may be identified as typically Indian. Again, the degree to which Indian features figure in the speech/writing of Indians varies from individual to individual.

Most people would agree that a standard variety of IE is close to native varieties. In fact, Dustoor (1968) and Krishnaswamy and Burde (1998) give samples of writing from India and other regions to demonstrate that it is not possible to identify IE. Schneider (2004) points out that there is no consensus as to the amount and nature of differences between native varieties of English. While some believe that there is great homogeneity, others think that there are perceivable differences.

Bauer (2002: 46) points out that it is difficult to identify grammatical features that distinguish a national variety even among native varieties of English. With corpora being available, preferences are identified rather than absolute differences. The same would then be the case for a non-native variety like IE. Besides, when it is a second language, it is always a language that is learnt and a prescriptive standard is set. If syntax is the sole criterion for arguing for or against a variety, as suggested by Krishnaswamy and Burde (1998), then varieties of native English also become suspect. When non-standard aspects are considered, the Indian features are so marked that one has to concede the existence of an Indian variety of English. So, the argument that there is no distinct IE that many put forward is untenable.

To repeat what was stated in Chapters 1 and 2, a distinction needs to be made between standard, non-standard and informal varieties and styles for IE as well. Non-standard IE tendencies creep into the standard. The morphosyntax of Indian English is also best placed on a cline. Standard Indian English insists on 'correctness'. While an Indian accent is acceptable, 'poor grammar' is quite unacceptable in most situations. Even those who argue for Indian English as a dialect in its own right will accept lexis and accents that are Indian but rarely grammar or syntax. As will be seen in the next chapter, lexis also does not have the same level of stigma that non-standard syntax does. This is unsurprising in the specific language situation of India.

The number of people who return English as their native language in the census as seen in Chapter 1 is very small. The number of those who actually believe that English is their first language is much larger than this but most of these people will not return English as their native language for purposes of census records. This is because they speak another language at home and that would determine their identity.

When a language is learnt as a second or a foreign language, the focus on 'correctness' is much greater than when the language under consideration is the native language. There are features that are Indian in Standard Indian English but usually native varieties become the benchmark for correctness. Standards could be British or American. Not surprisingly, most of the preferred, and taught, constructions are British rather than American. Since there is no written grammar for IE, in case of doubt, an English grammar is consulted.

It is further important to differentiate between what is standard, non-standard and informal. However, for some speakers of standard IE, non-standard forms appear in informal contexts. This is often a matter of convenience and sometimes a necessity, especially when interacting with someone who uses a non-standard variety.

Contrary to what Daswani (1978) says, Verma (1978) and Bhatt (2000, 2004) show that the features of IE that are considered to be non-standard are in fact regular and they can be accounted for by means of systematic rules. Moreover, speakers have intuitions about these non-standard structures. Bhatt (2000) claims that standard IE speakers have two grammars at their disposal – the standard and the non-standard.

3.1 Indian English – British or American?

In a study done by Kachru of faculty and student preferences with regard to the model of English that should be used in the education system in India, an overwhelming majority wanted BE—more than 65% of the faculty and students (Kachru 1976: 230). This is of course a rather old study and attitudes have changed considerably over the last three decades. The fact remains nevertheless that British models are considered to be the correct or best models for imparting English; attitudes are changing towards Americanisms, which were once frowned upon. IE is considered to be too sub-standard to be a good model to impart English.

Notwithstanding the debate on the differences between native varieties of English, there are works that specify the differences between AE and BE, such as Strevens (1972), Trudgill and Hannah (2002) and Algeo (2006).

Irrespective of the educators' view and the attitudes of people in general, it is observed that although English came from the British, there are some syntactic constructions in IE that are American. And, there is considerable variation in IE. Some structures are definitely British for all individuals. For example, in the following sentences *who* (British) is preferred to *that* (American):

23.

(a) The people who came yesterday...

(b) The people that came yesterday...

For some types of structures, both the British and the American forms are heard. For example, we find:

24.

(a) I insisted that she took the sweater. (British)

(b) I insisted that she take the sweater. (American)

25.

(a) We've just finished dinner. (British)

(b) We just finished dinner. (American)

IE has features of syntax that are predominantly British but there are structures that are American as well. In the use of *have* in standard IE, one comes across the different structures given in (26) below. A pilot study was conducted for this work and responses were gathered from forty proficient speakers of IE on their preferred structures. The test items here and those discussed below in 3.2.5 and the classification into British, American or both were taken from Trudgill and Hannah's

(2002) work. The respondents were from a wide age range from twenty-two years to seventy-seven years.[1] Among other questions, they were required to give their preferred structure between the two sentences:

26.

(a) Have you any coffee in the cupboard? (British)

(b) Do you have any coffee in the cupboard? (American)

The first sentence is said to be traditional British English and the second, American. The second form is more frequent today in BE also according to Trudgill and Hannah (2002). It turns out that, in IE as well, about 74% of the respondents prefer the second structure and this difference is not based on age. There is no significant difference across the different age groups. One might assume that BE would have a greater influence on older IE speakers but there are older respondents also who prefer the second structure and there are some younger respondents, including those in the age range of twenty to twenty-nine, who prefer the first structure.

Until recently, the emphasis on learning BE in the schools was very strong. However, we see strong American influences in the surveys done and this is also true at an impressionistic level. There are a variety of reasons for the different preferences. Indians read a lot of AE, especially fiction, and English-language films are generally from America rather than from Britain. Next, from the 1960s onward, many Indians have been educated and have worked in America, which is seen as a land of opportunity, with easier immigration laws than the UK.

From a historical perspective, it would be worthwhile to investigate, in the manner of Trudgill et al. (2002), whether the forms that match American patterns are relics of earlier British patterns. It is also necessary to do a more thorough investigation keeping in mind the type of schooling and the age of the informants before we can draw any serious conclusions regarding the British and American preferences of IE.

In other words, either there is free variation or there is contextual use of the different forms. This distinct possibility needs further investigation and such a study will establish more clearly what constitutes standard Indian English. In the end, what can be gathered is that IE has developed its own features and is neither British nor American. It has assimilated elements from both and has added its own as well. The findings reported as to the BE or AE preferences in IE in this section and below are admittedly based on a very small amount of data, and some amount of impressionistic observation, but standard IE does have its own character. Nobody disputes the Indian-ness of non-standard IE in any case.

Many of the IE features discussed below are non-standard in nature. Those items that are likely to be used in standard IE and those that are part of informal IE are pointed out for each structure described.

3.2 Verbs

Since verbs are at the heart of a sentence and determine, to a large extent, the nature of sentence structure, we begin with them.

3.2.1 Verb complements

It has been said by Mukherjee and Hoffmann (2006) that variation in syntax is most commonly realised in verb complement structures. That is, those elements that must obligatorily follow a verb in a sentence differ from variety to variety. In IE it is noted that some verbs that are normally transitive tend to be used intransitively. A transitive verb is one that obligatorily takes a noun or a complex noun after it in a sentence. An intransitive verb does not require any element after it obligatorily in a sentence. Other obligatory elements after a verb are adjectives and prepositional phrases.

Mukherjee and Hoffmann (2006) report one aspect of the work done on standard IE by Olavarria de Ersson and Shaw (2003) in which they contrast the use of the verb *pelt* and its complements in IE and in BE. Their study shows that the preference in BE is for this type of structure: verb + noun phrase (goal) + *with* noun phrase (*They are pelting him with cans.*). On the other hand, in IE there are more types used, the most frequent being this structure: verb + noun phrase + *at* noun phrase (goal) (*They are pelting cans at him.*).

Mukherjee and Hoffmann (2006) examine the frequencies of the ditransitive verbs *give* and *send* in BE and IE using the British and Indian sections of the International Corpus of English (Nelson 2007). A ditransitive verb is one that has two objects after it in a sentence:

27. Karuna gave Maya a book.

(Type I: verb + noun phrase (indirect object) + noun phrase (direct object))

The positions of the phrases following the verb can be changed in different ways:

> 28. Karuna gave a book to Maya.
>
> (Type II: verb + noun phrase (direct object) + *to* noun phrase (indirect object))

Sometimes, the complements of the verb can be omitted but the verb is still considered to be ditransitive since the objects are understood from the context or due to universal principles. Consequently, such structures as the following are also possible:

> 29.
>
> (a) Karuna gave a book.
>
> (Type III: verb + noun phrase (direct object) + null indirect object)
>
> (b) Karuna gave.
>
> (Type IV: verb + null indirect object + null direct object)
>
> (c) Karuna gave Maya.
>
> (Type V: verb + noun phrase (indirect object) + null direct object)

Of all these types, it is noted from a corpus-based study that, for the verb *give*, in BE, the greatest preference is for type I above whereas, in IE, the preference is for type III above in addition to other types. The same IE preference is noted for the ditransitive verb *send*.

The authors further say that, in the process of language change, verbs do change their grammatical properties even in native varieties of English and get grammatically institutionalised. Using a downloaded corpus of the archives of the Indian newspaper *The Statesman*, they note some verbs that have some degree of occurrence as type I ditransitive verbs – *advise, gift, present, provide* and *supply*. Of these, the most common is *provide* which is also possible in AE. None of these verbs is used as a type I occurrence in BE. The following illustrate the use of some of them as ditransitive verbs in IE.

> 30.
>
> (a) With an open-air cafeteria, the park would have provided the city the much-needed greenery.

(b) As a token of appreciation we presented each donor a travel bag and a certificate.

(c) The matter of quota reduction aside, the FCI is not supplying us the foodgrain for October and November.

(Adapted from Mukherjee and Hoffman 2006: 162)

The authors suggest that, considering its frequency of occurrence, the verb *gift* may have undergone a process of grammatical institutionalisation and become a ditransitive verb with type I occurrence in IE:

31. She said she wanted to gift him a dream.

(Mukherjee and Hoffman 2006: 163)

They suggest also that *advise* and *impart* are probably potential ditransitives in IE.

While the above are from standard IE, there are other instances of ditransitive use of verbs in non-standard IE such as *suggest* as in: *I will suggest you a solution.*

Use of verbs in non-standard IE typically converts transitive verbs into intransitives.

32.

(a) Ok, I'll take for transport. for Ok, I'll take money for transport.

(b) I didn't expect. for I didn't expect this.

In these cases, however, as in the case of ditransitives above, the noun is implied and the context suggests the noun. But, in the following example, the verb is genuinely used intransitively:

33. We enjoyed very much. for We enjoyed ourselves very much.

This phenomenon probably arises from the considerable elision that is permitted in Indian languages. This type of elision is heard in the informal speech of standard IE as well.

An earlier work on verb complementation is by Dixon (1991). He observes similar facts for IE and generalises the processes in some cases as follows. When two words with similar meanings are available to speakers of non-standard IE, they tend to use them in a single syntactic frame. That is, verbs like *agree* and *accept* have similar meanings but are used in different structures in standard IE: *Mary agreed to go* but *Mary accepted the invitation.* The verb *agree* is followed by a *to*-clause, whereas *accept* is followed by a noun phrase. Non-standard IE simply transfers *accept* into the syntactic frame of *agree* and thus constructs: *Mary accepted to go.*

Similarly, *want, wish, desire* and *hope* have similar meanings. Of these, *want* and *desire* take a noun phrase after them while *wish* and *hope* take a prepositional complement. The preposition required is *for*.

34.

(a) I want/desire a new car.

(b) I wish/hope for a new car.

In the questionnaire administered by Dixon in which respondents were to complete sentences with blanks, the tendency was to treat *wish, want* and *hope* exactly alike. Either all the answers of an individual contained a noun phrase directly after the verb or all had *for* uniformly after them. Sometimes, *hope* was treated differently (as *hope for*) but the other verbs had no preposition after them. Thus the responses were:

35.

(a) I wish a promotion in my job

(b) I want a promotion in my job.

(Dixon 1991: 444)

Further, a *to*-complement is possible with all these verbs but only *wish, desire* and *hope* permit a *that*-clause after them. However, in non-standard IE *want* is used with a *that*-clause in sentences like *I want that I should get it* by analogy with the other verbs.

The desire to use high-sounding words in the style of IE – that is, using Romance vocabulary of English (of French and Latin origin) – or a less common Germanic word rather than the more common Germanic words has also been noted. Subramanian (1978), for example, illustrates the preference of Indians for an overly expressive style of writing – a style that is considered to be poetic. Dixon (1991) comments that this proclivity combined with the use of one syntactic frame for words with similar meanings has some of the following results. The syntactic frame of these sentences is more appropriate for the verb in brackets rather than the verb actually used in the sentence.

36.
- (a) It inhabits in all kinds of habitats. (live)
- (b) He discussed about the job. (talk)
- (c) They conceived about it. (think)
- (d) They reached to Bombay. (come)
- (e) He presented me a gift. (give)
- (f) I require to be lent some money. (need)
- (g) I requested you whether you would read my essay. (ask)
- (h) I demanded him to do it. (ask)

(Adapted from Dixon 1991: 445–6)

3.2.2 Verb Particles

The addition of the particle *off* to almost any verb to intensify it is quite common across the country. The verb *marry off* is possible in native varieties and in standard IE in a sentence like:

37. They married off their daughter against her wishes.

In IE, the additional sense in which it would be used is 'actually did it' as in:

38. She married off without her parents' consent.

Almost any transitive verb can be used with this sense:

39.
- (a) I'll eat it off.
- (b) I'll write off. 'I'll finish writing (and be done with it)' *contra* 'give up on'
- (c) I'll finish it off.

A credit card company brings this aspect of IE into focus with 'You fuel your vehicle, we'll waive off the surcharge' in an advertisement. It will be seen in *marry off* in (38) above that the verb may also be used intransitively. An example of an intransitive verb used with *off* is:

    40. I'll sleep off.   'I'll go off to sleep.'

Notice in (39) that, when a pronoun occurs, the particle *off* appears after it, as is the case with other particles in standard English:

    41.

    (a) They called him up.

    (b) *They called up him.

    (c) They called up Prakash.

    (d) They called Prakash up.

However, there are speakers who will not split the verb and the particle even in sentences that contain a pronoun.

    42.

    (a) They called up him.

    (b) Suresh rang up him.

This difference depends on the proficiency of the speaker and is non-standard use. Items in (42) above are not possible even in informal speech of standard IE speakers, whereas items with *off* (39) would be heard in the informal speech of speakers of Standard IE.

Another common particle in IE usage is *out*:

    43.

    (a) My secretary will fair out the written draft.   'make a fair copy'

    (b) We can't make out what's being said.   'understand'

3.2.3 The progressive

In non-standard IE the progressive (that is the *-ing* form of a verb) is used quite freely. As a result, verbs that cannot be used with *-ing* such as *have* (in the sense of possessing) are used in the progressive form:

44.

(a) I am having three books with me.

(b) I am liking it.

(c) You may be knowing it.

(d) She is not understanding anything.

While these would be classified as non-standard, there is an overall tendency in all varieties of IE to use the progressive form. Sentences with the progressive form are more commonly used than the ones without in the list given below:

45.

(a) I am enclosing copies of my certificates.   I enclose copies of my certificates.

(b) I am attaching a file to this letter.   I attach a file to this letter.

3.2.4 Tense concord (absent)

When a sentence is complex, the tense across the clauses often does not match as it does in native varieties of English.

46.

IE	Native varieties
(a) He said he will attend classes.	He said he would attend classes.
(b) Girish thought that he will pass.	Girish thought that he would pass.
(c) Chitra predicted that she can do it.	Chitra predicted that she could do it.

In general, the principle is that, if the second event described by the sentence is either in present or future time, then the past tense is not used in the second clause. Many users of standard IE also tend not to maintain inter-clausal tense agreement.

Another common feature of non-standard IE is the use of the present perfect aspect – that is, use of the auxiliary verb *have* with the main verb — instead of the simple past along with an adverb that specifies time.

47.

(a) I have seen this movie last year. 'I saw this movie last year.'

(b) Sita has returned home in the evening. 'Sita returned home in the evening.'

(c) I have returned the book to the library two weeks back. 'I returned the book to the library two weeks ago.'

3.2.5 Auxiliary verbs

Some work has been done on the use of modals in IE. Shastri (1988) reports a study done by Katikar (1984) on the use of modals in which it is claimed that there is no significant difference in the way modals are used in IE compared with native varieties. Wilson (2005), in a study that relates the use of modals to the genre in which they are used, corroborates the claim made by Katikar that there are few significant differences between varieties in the use of modals.

Katikar's work also finds that the frequency of the past forms *would* and *could* is higher and this too results in tense concord across clauses not being maintained. The higher incidence of the past forms may be attributed to the impression that they contribute to greater politeness in discourse. Thus we find sentences in which *would* and *could* are used in which *will* and *can* are more acceptable in standard IE.

48.

(a) Attached to this you would find my answers.

(b) Paid accommodation could be arranged on request.

Another finding of Katikar's study is the higher frequency of *shall* in the corpus and this is seen as a consequence of the influence of written English over spoken English in India.

In the pilot study conducted on the use of auxiliary verbs for the current work, forty informants were asked to fill in the blanks choosing from the options given to them. The options were a British form, an American form or a form that is common to both BE and AE. Different combinations were presented to the respondents. They were not given the details regarding usage. All items were drawn from Trudgill and Hannah (2002).[2] Some examples are:

49

(a) I _____ tell you later. (*shall*: BE and *will* BE and AE)

(b) When I was young, I _____ there every day. (*went*: BE, *used to go*: BE and AE; *would go*: AE)

(c) I wish I _____ done it. (*had*: BE and AE, *would have*: AE)

(d) You _____ have said that. (*ought not to*: BE, *shouldn't*: AE).

Or they were asked to choose between two structures:

50.

(a) Do you need to be so rude? (BE and AE)

(b) Need you be so rude? (BE)

A total of fourteen items were tested in this fashion. The total possible number of BE responses in the questionnaire was twelve; the total American responses was five; and the BE and AE responses was twelve. Aggregating the first preference given by the forty respondents, the following picture emerges: most of the responses were for the common BE and AE forms at 70.2%, as against 26% for American and 34.58% for British forms. These results show that the core treatment of auxiliary verbs is common across the nations. Of the remaining, IE seems to have a slight tilt towards BE forms over AE but this could be due to the greater number of items with a BE response in the questionnaire. Again, there are no particular differences across age groups.

This survey also reveals that the same individual is likely to use both the American and the British variety in different contexts or on different occasions. Some respondents comment that the use of a form would also be determined by the context and that they would use *shall* in a more formal context and *will* in a less formal one.

It is quite common to see modals and other auxiliaries being used tautologically in a sentence and this phenomenon may be related to the conjoined phrases that is noted below (3.7). An example of tautology is 'Perhaps that may be one of the reasons that castles in Japan rise above circlets of misty pink sakura' (Santanagopalan 2007: 8).

3.3 Articles

Non-standard IE is frequently commented on for the manner in which the articles – *a, an, the* – are used. The ability to use articles in the manner of a native speaker may be said to be one of the markers of proficiency in English. A great deal of writing appears on this use of articles. It must be borne in mind that standard IE makes use of articles very much in the fashion of native varieties. Other than that, speakers tend to use articles where they are not necessary and leave them out where they are. Some of the empirical works on article use are Agnihotri et al. (1984) and, more recently, Sand (2004), and Sharma (2005). In Sand (2004), a study of article use based on corpora of different varieties of English is reported. The author argues that there is variation in article use across different text types. Particularly significant is the observation that native varieties of English also show variation in article use, a point illustrated in Trudgill and Hannah (2002: 72–3) as well. Consequently, such use is likely to be interpreted differently in non-native varieties of English which are overtly learnt.

Dixon (1991) recounts a story, narrated to him by Professor R. A. Kelkar, of a student in whose writing the use of articles was bizarre. The student explained this use by stating that after writing the essay without any articles at all, she felt that some articles ought to be there and added them in a random fashion. Dixon suggests that, as a consequence and in spite of the several lists prepared by scholars of article misuse, it is not really possible to generalise on IE article use.

Putting aside the different reasons for variable article use that these works discuss, some specific types of non-standard uses seen in IE are identified below. In the first instance, an article is missing where it should appear.

51.

(a) What is wrong with watch?   (when specifying a particular one)

(b) Where is ghee?   (*ghee* 'clarified butter')

The indefinite article *a/an* is absent in the following:

52.

(a) We had group discussion.

(b) We saw Telugu film *Boss*.

These sentences are constructed probably because, in general, the noun that is to be modified is uncountable. This is extended to contexts in which it is to be treated as a countable one. In the example (52b), the rule that proper nouns do not take an article before them is extended to the qualified noun as well.

The definite article *the* appears in the examples below where a collective noun with a generic meaning occurs:

53.

   (a) Man should learn to live amicably in the society.

   (b) The people...

   (c) The girls and the boys...

Idioms also tend to get Indianised in the use of articles:

54.

   (a) Back to the square one.

   (b) Eat the cake and have it too.

   (c) Play it by the ear.

More examples are available in Dustoor (1968); see also Sample 4 in Chapter 7. This non-standard use of articles generally does not percolate into standard speech but may be heard in the spontaneous speech of those who speak standard IE. Article use is probably among the last features to be learnt or the most difficult to acquire (Sharma 2005).

3.4 Topicalisation

In a sentence, when an item is being discussed, it is often placed at the beginning and the details about it are given after it. As Bhatt (2004) notes, different items can be brought to the beginning of a sentence. It is quite common in IE for the adverbial indicating place, time and other additional information to be placed at the beginning of a sentence rather than at the end.

55.

   (a) Recently, we found a question paper.

   (b) Yesterday, I went to see a movie.

   (c) In the park, the bombs were placed.

   (d) At four o' clock, the movie begins.

It is not merely adverbials that move to the beginning of the sentence. Unexpectedly, even objects in a sentence get fronted:

56.
  (a) Five minutes I am not getting.
  (b) This book I will return tomorrow.
  (c) That you told me.

This type of construction is very common and is contrary to the normal sentence structure of English that places the objects after the verb as in:

57.
  (a) I am not getting five minutes.
  (b) I will return this book tomorrow.
  (c) You told me that.

While the sentences in (57) are common to standard and non-standard IE, the ones in (56) above are quite common in non-standard speech. They are also found in informal contexts of standard speech. They would, however, not be acceptable in written contexts.

Bhatt (2004) further notes that it is possible to bring forward the topic even in embedded or complex structures such as the following:

58.
  (a) His friends know that her parents, he doesn't like at all. 'His friends know that he doesn't like her parents at all.'
  (b) Papa-ji only told us that their money, he will not touch. 'Papa-ji told us that that he will not touch their money.'
  (c) My brother warned me that young boys I should say no to. 'My brother warned me that I should say no to young boys.'

(Adapted from Bhatt 2004: 1023)

There are other related examples but with more complex processes involved:

59.
  (a) Bees, the way they communicate with each other, is an excellent example of this sort of communication.
  (b) Two years she took leave. 'She took leave for two years.'

Example (59a) comes from a student's script.

3.5 *only*

The use of *only* in non-standard IE is interesting. Bhatt (2000, 2004) gives a detailed linguistic description of focus placement. Here, another aspect of non-standard IE use of *only* is illustrated.

60.

(a) The teacher sent an email only to the students. (not something else)

(b) The teacher sent an email to the students only. (not to others)

In these sentences, *only* appears after the element that is emphasised. In (60a), however, there is a slight pause after *only* and before *to the students*. Based on facts such as these Bhatt presents generalisations regarding focus placement, stating that it is at the right edge. In standard IE the equivalent sentences would be:

61.

(a) The teacher sent only an email to the students.

(b) The teacher sent an email only to the students.

Bhatt also notes another phenomenon with regard to the placement of *only*. Contrary to norms in standard varieties of English, the verb and its complement can be separated by an adverb when an element is being focussed:

62.

(a) These women wear everyday expensive clothes only. (emphasis on expensive clothes, not contrasting with anything else)

(b) He will buy over there tickets, only. (emphasis on tickets, not contrasting with anything else)

(Adapted from Bhatt 2004: 1024)

This type of focus is not contrastive but is called presentational by Bhatt. In presentational focus, the subject noun phrase is also focused in its own position:

63.

(a) These women only said this.

(b) The teacher only sent an email.

The use of *only* illustrated in (61 and 62) above is absent in standard IE and is ridiculed by other Indians with the statement: 'Indians, we are like this only.'

Another use of *only* is seen in sentences like the following:

64.

(a) The light bulb didn't work only.

(b) Some people don't give only.

(c) Those communities don't take only.

In these cases, *only* has the meaning of *at all*. In standard English, these sentences mean:

65.

(a) The light bulb didn't work at all.

(b) Some people don't give (anything) at all.

(c) Those communities don't take (anything) at all.

Another usage similar to the use of *only* is the use of *even* at the end of a sentence:

66. I am not getting five minutes even. 'I am not getting even five minutes.'

3.6 Question formation

3.6.1 Wh- questions

Standard IE follows native patterns in questions. That is, when a question is formed using *wh*-words, it is assumed to be constructed out of a statement. Thus, *Where are you going?* is created from *You are going where* by moving *where* to the beginning of the sentence and by inverting the positions of the subject *you* and the verb *are*. Other examples from Standard IE are:

67.

(a) When will you begin?   from   You will begin when?

(b) What are you reading?   from   You are reading what?

(c) Why are you crying?   from   You are crying why?

(d) How will you come?   from   You will come how?

While the set in (67) above is correct in standard IE, non-standard IE follows a different pattern. Instead of two different processes happening in question formation, in non-standard IE, only one happens. The question word is moved to the front of the sentence but the inversion of the subject and verb does not take place. Thus non-standard IE has the following structures:

68.

(a) When you will begin?

(b) What you are reading?

(c) Why you are crying?

(d) How you will come?

As noted by Bhatt (2000, 2004) another process happens when the question is indirect – that is, when the clause that contains the question is embedded. In Standard IE as in other varieties, although the *wh-* word is brought to the beginning of the embedded clause, there is no inversion of the subject and the verb.

69.

(a) We asked when you would begin.   from   We asked you would begin when.

(b) They know where you are going.   from   They know you are going where.

In non-standard IE, on the other hand, inversion does take place:

70.

(a) We asked when would you begin.

(b) They know where are you going.

Another interesting feature of non-standard IE that is also transferred to standard informal speech is the use of *wh-* questions beginning with *where* as a rhetorical device to suggest that the event is not happening:

71.

    (a) Where are you sleeping?   'You are not sleeping at all.'

    (b) Where is he coming?   'He is not coming at all.'

    (c) Where is he studying?   'He is not studying at all.'

Another favourite Indian expression is *What to do?* meaning 'We cannot do anything about it.' *What all things we do* suggests 'The things we do!'

3.6.2 Yes-no questions

Questions that require either *yes* or *no* as an answer are constructed in standard IE as in native varieties of English. The questions are said to be derived from sentences by a process of inverting the positions of the subject and the auxiliary verb. In cases where there is no auxiliary and the verb is a form of *be* the main verb is inverted with the subject. In all other cases, another auxiliary verb *do* is introduced.

72.

(a)	Will you come?	from	You will come.
(b)	Is Ganesh at home?	from	Ganesh is at home.
(c)	Are you waiting?	from	You are waiting.
(d)	Did he sleep well?	from	He slept well.
(e)	Does Rekha seem happy?	from	Rekha seems happy.
(f)	Did Gopi write to him?	from	Gopi wrote to him.

However, the predominant tendency in standard as well as non-standard IE is to not invert the subject and auxiliary as above. The preference is to retain the structure of the statement and to use a rising intonation pattern on the sentence:

73.

    (a) You will come?

    (b) Ganesh is at home?

    (c) You are waiting?

    (d) He slept well?

(e) Rekha seems happy?

(f) Gopi wrote to him?

3.6.3 Tag questions

Standard IE follows native varieties of English in the use of tag questions.

74.

(a) You will come, won't you?

(b) You can come tomorrow, can't you?

(c) They should do it, shouldn't they?

Non-standard IE on the other hand, exhibits the invariant tag *isn't it?* in all contexts (see for example Trudgill and Hannah 2002).

75.

(a) You will come, isn't it?

(b) You can come tomorrow, isn't it?

(c) They should do it, isn't it?

In addition to this, non-standard IE also uses the invariant *no* as a tag.

76.

(a) You will come, no?

(b) You can come tomorrow, no?

(c) They should do it, no?

If degrees of non-standardness are set up, *no* is lower on the scale (see also Chapter 4).

3.7 Reduplication, reduced phrases, fused phrases

It is quite common for non-standard IE to use reduplication to indicate several items of the same quality or to emphasise the quality that is being described.

77.

   (a) We need little-little things to fill up this space.

   (b) There are many small-small holes in this dress.

   (c) It's all sticky-sticky.

   (d) We brought the children some lovely-lovely clothes.

The preference in reduplication is to use mono- or disyllabic words. In the sentences above, both number and quality are indicated.

A related process involving numerals in particular is also seen. Such phrases are often used in place of full phrases that would be conjoined with *or*. We may call them reduced phrases.

78.

   (a) I was eleven-twelve years old.   'I was eleven or twelve years old.'

   (b) Get some three-four books.   'Get three or four books.'

   (c) Give me two-three minutes.   'Give me two or three minutes.'

In these examples, the number is not fixed and the phrase suggests a range. Another type of example is the following:

79. In my childhood, we had two-two cars.   'In my childhood, we had two cars (when most people had none).'

In (79), however, the number is fixed and is indicative of contrast and emphasis.

The degree to which these would appear in standard IE varies. The reduplicative elements given in (77) are heard in standard IE as well. The sentences (78a–c) are less likely to be heard in standard IE but are not completely ruled out. They are certainly likely to be heard in informal contexts.

A few sporadic elements are presented now of items which appear to be fused phrases constructed as a result of input forms of a similar nature.

80.

   (a) If you can able to wait...   'If you are able to wait.' or 'If you can wait.'

(b) I could not able to do it. 'I could not do it.' or 'I was not able to do it.'

(c) Why because... 'Why? Because...'

(d) If suppose... 'If...'; 'Suppose...'

(e) You need not to worry. 'You don't need to worry.' or 'You need not worry.'

These items seem to be mergers of related phrases. The precise nature of merger needs to be examined in detail. These are, however, quite low on the scale of non-standardness and would not be heard from a speaker of standard IE.

3.8 Prepositions

Prepositions are often used differently in non-standard IE from standard IE. These are literal translations of the corresponding structures in Indian languages:

81.

(a) What did you do to us? 'What did you do for us?'

(b) I got angry on him. 'I got angry at him.'

(c) You are entitled for free tickets 'You are entitled to free tickets.'

An advertisement goes, 'If a picture can speak thousands of words, imagine what a video can do to your business' where the intended meaning is that a video would aid in improving the business.

3.9 Idioms

Despite serious attention to idioms and metaphors in school, comfortable use of idioms is rare. What is typical of non-standard IE is the literal translation of Indian idioms into English. Thus we find expressions such as:

82.

(a) He will eat my brain 'He will harangue me.'

(b) My client had to drink seven tanks of water. 'My client underwent torment.'

(c) I hit my own feet with the hammer. 'I damaged my own interests.'

(d) He has brains in the knee cap. 'He has no brains at all.'

These are translations from different Indian languages. The first example which seems to have become part of non-standard IE is from Hindi, the rest are translations from Telugu. They are often used in jest and are not conventionalised.

3.10 Code-switching

A very common feature of the multilingual situation of India is that of code-switching.[3] Code-switching is the phenomenon of beginning an utterance in one language and changing the language mid-course. Code-switching occurs at various levels – the word, the sentence and at the level of discourse. This usually happens in an informal context. Code-switching in Hindi-English is the most commonly discussed topic in India – see, for example, Singh (1985), Kumar (1986) and Pandit (1986). Some constraints have been stated in the literature on code-switching – it has been said that shifts between languages are possible only in certain places and not just about anywhere. A detailed discussion of the theoretical aspects is beyond the scope of this work.

As early as 1936, Chib observes that a lawyer may be heard saying in court: '*Yeh* argument water *nahin* hold *kardi hai*' – 'This argument does not hold water.' – mixing English, Urdu and Punjabi. Chib believes that this phenomenon is due to the fact that 'thoughts are unconsciously being translated into different modes of speech' (Chib 1936: 54).

Some examples of Hindi-English code-switching in sentences gathered from spontaneous speech are:

83.

(a) There is no other raasta for this problem.

   'way'

'There is no other way for this problem.'

(b) Have your tea aur jaldi chalo.

   'and fast come'

'Have your tea and come fast.'

(c) Why does she give the impression kii she has learnt Odissi?

   'that'

'Why does she give the impression that she has learnt Odissi?'

(d) If you intend to come to my place toh apne saamaan leke aao.

'then your luggage bring come'

'If you intend to come to my place then bring your luggage and come.'

(e) Fikar not.

'worry'

'Don't worry.'

(Adapted from Suman 2007: 54–6)

Code-switching is quite common in advertisements, songs, film dialogues, gossip columns in newspapers and magazines, chat shows on radio and television and on various billboards and in everyday speech. Kachru (2006) demonstrates the use of code-switching in pop culture, specifically in songs in Hindi films. Bhatia (1987) presents an analysis of code-switched advertisements from Hindi-English in terms of their discourse content.

3.11 Inflectional forms

Many English verbs have the same form for the past and the past participle. Thus a verb like *play* is *played* in the past – *I played the new game* – and also in the past participle form – *I have already played the new game.* Irregular verbs, on the other hand, have different forms for the past and the participle – for *swim*, *swam* and *swum*. There are some differences though between BE and AE in this regard. Generally, and as may be expected, IE follows BE. But again there are some exceptions which are made clear in (84) below. The British and American verbs below are from Trudgill and Hannah (2002: 56). The abbreviations p and pp stand for the past and past participle respectively.

84.

	AE	BE	IE
dream	dreamed	dreamt	dreamt
kneel	kneeled	knelt	knelt
lean	leaned	leant	leaned
leap	leaped	leapt	leapt

In (84) above there is a change in the vowel quality in the past and participle form in BE and IE.

85.

	AE	BE	IE
burn	burned	burnt	burnt
dwell	dwelled	dwelt	dwelt (rare)
learn	learned	learnt	learnt
smell	smelled	smelt	smelt
spell	spelled	spelt	spelt
spill	spilled	spilt	spilt
spoil	spoiled	spoilt	spoilt

In (85), the vowel quality remains but the irregular verb is regularised in AE.

86.

	AE	BE	IE
dive	dove (p), dived (pp)	dived	dived
fit	fit (p), fitted (pp)	fitted	fitted
sneak	snuck (p, pp)	sneaked	sneaked
get	got (p), gotten (pp)	got	got

In (86) it is the American verbs that are more irregular.

The above examples demonstrate that, except perhaps for one word, *leaned*, the IE forms correspond more to the BE forms. Such words as *dwell* and *dive* are rarely used in IE.

Some nouns in Indian English are used as plurals whereas in native varieties they would be classified as uncountable and, therefore, not able to be pluralised at all – for example, *furnitures, moneys, feedbacks, equipments* etc. Thus uncountable nouns become countable. It is also possible for a person to say *an equipment, a furniture* rather than *a piece of equipment/furniture*.

The reverse of this – that is, words always used in the plural – are used in the singular – *pant, scissor, sprout*. Thus for example, *Give me a scissor* is not uncommon. *I will have a sprout* for *a bowl of sprouts* is heard in a canteen. Or items such as *news* become countable – 'I want to share a good news with you.'

Often, there are words that are used in a different category from the one they belong to in standard IE. For example, *Sents* is a folder in an Indian email service. It is not uncommon to hear or read *This tantamounts to a joke.* All of these usages are completely non-standard.

Code-switching happens with inflections also: *moguds and pellams* 'husbands and wives' is the name of a Telugu film. The English plural inflectional -*s* is attached to Indian words. The difference between what we have called non-standard and these structures is that these may be used in informal contexts by users of standard IE as well.

However, the chance of these code-switched informal structures becoming a part of standard IE is less than the chance of the non-standard forms becoming standardised. Just as it is claimed here that the standard form of IE is pan-Indian, crucially, Verma (1978) points out the features that are identified as non-standard are also pan-Indian and are not restricted to some regions of the country. There are region-specific features which are not touched upon here.

An important point brought out by Mukherjee and Hoffmann (2006) is that there is standardisation of at least one verb structure in IE. The authors acknowledge the need for a diachronic study as well for what they call institutionalisation; the significant point is that standardisation of what are considered to be non-standard is happening.

The point made by Bhatt (2000) that Indians move from standard IE to the non-standard routinely is not as simple as it is made out to be because many non-standard features of IE would never be used by some speakers of standard IE.

Syntax, like phonology, illustrates the point that standard and non-standard in IE are not water-tight compartments, even though there is greater emphasis on correctness here, both by way of expectation and in teaching.

Notes

1. Twenty-three respondents were between the ages of twenty and twenty-nine years; thirteen in the range of thirty to thirty-nine; and 4 in the range of forty-plus.
2. Finer distinctions such as older and younger British and informal American were not taken into account in the analysis. The American construction *I wish I would have done it* is considered to be recent, informal and spoken by Trudgill and Hannah (2002). This structure would be non-standard in IE.
3. D'souza (1992) discusses the issue of whether code-switching is an essential component of new varieties of English and concludes that it is not. The distinction between code-switching and code-mixing is also discussed in the same article.

4 Lexis and Discourse

Lexis of Indian English has been studied to some extent by scholars. Since early times, words that have gone from India to native varieties of English have been of scholarly and general interest. When compared to syntax, the insistence on the use of the standard form is less pressing for lexis. There are definitely words that are considered to be standard and others non-standard, while some are considered to be informal. These are discussed in this chapter. Discourse, as may be expected, draws from features of Indian languages.

4.1 Indian English Lexis

There is substantial creativity in Indian English lexis. There are different ways in which the vocabulary of Indian English has been built up. But, before we consider those aspects, it will be useful to do a little comparison with native varieties first and also to look at what constitutes Indian English lexis.

4.1.1 British, American and Indian

A corpus-based study of British (Lancaster-Oslo/Bergen Corpus), American (Brown Corpus) and Indian English (The Kolhapur Corpus) reveals a core vocabulary of a little over 1000 words (Geisler 2000) across the varieties. In IE, many words that have no cultural or other kinds of significance are either not used or are rare, irrespective of whether they are from Britain or USA. Some examples are:

> 87.
> snow plough
> smog
> garter
> suspender

jumper
pantyhose/tights

The words above, however, are familiar to those who are even moderately well-read.

IE lexis, like morphosyntax discussed in the previous chapter, is largely British but there are some preferences for American words. Comparing the different forms from Trudgill and Hannah (2002), we find that some words from USA are preferred in India. Some examples are:

88.

IE/AE	BE
stove	cooker
pharmacy	chemist
hardware store	ironmonger
buffet	sideboard

The American *faculty* is preferred in Indian universities over the British *staff*. In Indian universities, *staff* refers to non-teaching staff. The word *staff* is not rejected and is more commonly used in colleges and schools rather than universities.

British words are used instead of the American equivalents in the following list:

89.

IE/BE	AE
jam	jelly
jelly	jello
jug	pitcher
lorry	truck
dustbin	garbage can
tap	faucet
petrol	gas
pavement	sidewalk

In general, most of IE lexis comes from Britain. However, several words are completely different from both British and American English:

90.

IE	BE/AE
brinjal	aubergine/eggplant
lady's finger	okra
wine shop	off-licence/liquor store

dickey	boot/trunk
metro	underground railway
torchlight	torch

Sweater is a term for all kinds of warm clothing worn over other clothes; *purse* must be held in the hand; and *handbag* must have handles and be slung on the shoulder.

4.1.2 Indian meanings

Some English words have meanings that are quite different from the meanings in native varieties. For example:

91.

IE	meaning
stir	'strike'
shift	'move, especially house or office'
clever	'intelligent, especially cunning'
smart	'well-dressed' or 'cunning'
bearer	'waiter'
back-bencher	'one who occupies the last rows in a classroom, generally a dull or mischievous student'
botheration	'bother'
quarters	'houses owned by government or employer and allocated to employees for residence'
hotel	'restaurant'
mythological	'a film with a mythological theme'
social	' a film with a social theme'
latrine	'a toilet in any place'
mixture	'a snack combining several ingredients, such as lentils and peanuts'
convent	'a school run by Christians'

It is important to make a distinction between acceptable Indian meanings and inappropriate use of words that one comes across repeatedly in India, which would be considered non-standard or would constitute improper understanding of the meaning of a word.

92.

(a) Use gems, improve your love-life, become star-crossed lovers.

(b) He has improvised in his studies.

(c) I hope your car is giving trouble.

In (92a), the intended meaning is that by using gems, the love-life of individuals would improve but the incorrect use of *star-crossed* gives the opposite meaning. In (92b), the intended word is *improve* and, in (91c), *hope* is used incorrectly instead of *think*.

4.2 Indian influence on English

The only feature that distinguishes Indian English from other varieties of English more than lexis is phonology. While phonology is necessarily spoken, lexis is a feature of both spoken and written English. English, as is well known, is very assimilative of the different languages of the world.

4.2.1 Assimilated items

Given Britain's prolonged contact with India, a number of Indian words have become a part of the English lexicon. That is, these are words that are used in IE as well as native varieties of English, especially British English, and also perhaps in other varieties of English. The process started even earlier than the colonial period, with Old English itself. Some Sanskrit words, such as *pepper,* went to English through Greek and Latin. The word *sandal* 'sandalwood' (from Sanskrit *candana*) is found as early as 1400 (Serjeantson 1935: 221). With the coming of the Europeans in the fifteenth century and later during the colonial period, the process of borrowing from Indian languages became intense. Those words that have become part of native varieties of English are called assimilated items. Some of the words have gone directly into English while others have been assimilated into English through other (European) languages such as Portuguese and French. The process of taking Indian words into English is a continuing one and is even more prominent in the modern, globalised world. Most of the words undergo phonological and semantic changes in the process of transfer.

Serjeantson (1935) provides a classificatory list of the Indian words that have become assimilated into English from the earliest times of contact between Britain and India. Subba Rao (1954) also provides a word list from the seventeenth century onwards. Some of the more common words seen in English from the sixteenth century are:

93.
lac	'resin', from Sanskrit
divan	from Persian
caravan	from Persian, perhaps through French
calico	from the name Calicut, in Kerala

betel — from Malayalam, through Portuguese
coir — from Malayalam, through Portuguese
curry — from Tamil

Words of the seventeenth century are:

94.
guru
pundit
chintz
punch (the drink)
cot
bungalow
juggernaut
pukka

All the above are from Hindustani.

95.
mongoose — from Marathi
sepoy — from Persian
shawl — from Persian
pariah — from Tamil
cheroot — from Tamil
catamaran — from Tamil
teak — from Malayalam, through Portuguese

Some eighteenth-century words are:

96.
cheetah
chit
bangle
shampoo
nautch

All of these are from Hindustani.

97.
avatar — from Sanskrit
jute — from Bengali
corundum — from Tamil

mulligatawny	from Tamil
bandicoot	from Telugu

Words seen in English from the nineteenth century are:

98.
dacoit
thug
cashmere
pyjamas
chutney
loot
gymkhana
pug

All of the above are again from Hindustani.

99.
yoga	from Sanskrit
maya	from Sanskrit
karma	from Sanskrit
khaki	from Persian
patchouli	from Tamil

As may be expected, words are taken from a particular register en masse especially when corresponding vocabulary is missing in the borrowing language. One such register is philosophy. Words such as *avatar, guru, dharma, karma, moksha* etc. have been taken from Indian philosophy into English and have no original English equivalents. Most words borrowed during the nineteenth century are from philosophy (Serjeantson 1935: 221).

In the end however, considering the long association between Britain and India, only a small number of Indian words have actually passed into English vocabulary. The reason for this is that India never became a white man's country. Subba Rao (1954) says that this was due to the climate. This, however, is debatable. Those Britons who came to India carried back wealth and tales of an exotic land and the vocabulary was, to a large extent, incomprehensible. Correspondence between the British in India and Britian reveals exasperation on the part of those 'back home' towards the incomprehensibility of the language used and highlights the need for some kind of glossary.

Every fortnight brings a mail from India, and the intelligence it imparts is fraught with words which perplex the multitude... The new arrival in India, ignorant of the language of the country, is puzzled, for some time to comprehend his countrymen, whose conversation 'wears strange suits', and even he, who has been for years a sojourner in India is, to the last, unacquainted with the meaning of numerous words which occur in his daily newspaper, the Courts of law, and the communications of his Mofussil or up-country correspondents (Stocqueler 1920: iii).

During the Raj, it became necessary for the British in India to understand local languages for proper administration. The adoption of local vocabulary was mostly due to need and, to some extent, it was seen as affectation by Serjeantson (1935) and Subba Rao (1954). The need to communicate with the local people led to the preparation of a number of glossaries and lexicons for different purposes – for example, those by Wilson in 1855 and by Whitworth in 1885 – and they were meant for administration and general communication. Yule and Burnell published what is perhaps the first dictionary of colloquial items in 1886. This work is better known than the others and has the deliberately catchy title of *Hobson-Jobson*.

4.2.2 Restricted items

What marks Indian English today are those items that have not made it into native varieties of English. Not all the words recorded in the early dictionaries mentioned above were assimilated into British English. Subba Rao points out that, of the 26,000 words in Wilson's dictionary, most have remained unknown outside the subcontinent. In fact, not all of the words have remained in use in India. Some examples of words that are no longer used today are: *failsoof* 'an artful dodger', *calaluz* 'swift rowing vessel', *keddah* 'to chase or hunt'.

These words and dictionaries were initially required for proper communication between the local people and the British administrators. Subsequently, a huge stock of Indian words developed for modern India which is used today. No comprehensive dictionary of Indian English words is available in modern times. *The Advanced Oxford Learner's Dictionary* prepared an Indian English supplement to its fifth edition (Sengupta 1996). Later editions do not contain this supplement. The *Advanced Oxford* is one of several small attempts at making available the lexical items without which reading or understanding Indian English becomes difficult. Hawkins (1984) and Muthiah (1991) are similar works.

All these dictionaries face the problem of establishing words that are universally accepted in India. The primary reason for the difficulty lies in the existence of several languages. Many words are region-specific and are not pan-Indian. As Serjeantson (1935) notes for assimilated words, by far the largest number of Indian words in Indian English are from Hindi/Hindustani. Fewer words from other languages have found acceptance at the national level. Some of the words taken from Hindi/Hindustani are:

100.
bandh	'a closure of all shops and institutions in a place'
crore	'ten million'
hartal	'a strike'
gherao	'to surround an official to prevent movement'
henna/mehendi	'a natural dye used decoratively on hands and hair'
shamiana	'decorative tarpaulin made of cloth'
dharna	'a sit-in'

Words specific to certain registers or relating to the culture of the land are part of the restricted items, used only in India. Some examples from the arts are:

101.
abhinaya	'expression in dance'
raga	'patterned melody in Indian music'
tala	'patterned beat in Indian music'
aasana	'yogic posture'

Religion:

102.
aarti	'ritual offering of camphor flame to a deity'
puja	'ritual prayer'
hundi	'receptacle for offerings mostly in temples'
sadhvi	'woman spiritual aspirant'
sadhaka	'male spiritual aspirant'
darga(h)	'a tomb of a Muslim or Sufi saint'

Food items:

103.
chikki	'fudge made usually with peanuts'
bhel puri	'item in Indian fast food'

khichdi	'rice and lentil dish'
maida	'refined flour'
chota	'small, in particular, a measure of alcohol'

Miscellaneous items:

104.

challan	'pay-in slip'
acharya	'teacher of high standing'
agarbatti	'joss stick'
achcha	'good, OK'
chaalu	'cunning'
baccha	'novice'
dhaba	'road-side eatery'
hungama	'commotion'
kabaddi	'Indian version of the game Tag'
kadai	'deep frying pan'
kho-kho	'Indian game'

Clothing:

105.

kurta	'long, loose Indian shirt'
salwar-kameez	'loose pyjamas with a long top commonly worn by women'
dupatta/chunni	'scarf used with salwar kameez'

Most of the words above are from Hindi/Urdu and a few are from Sanskrit. Words from other languages do not make it to the national level as easily as Hindi words do. Some examples of those that have are:

106.

shikakai	'vegetable extract used for washing hair'
rasam	'mulligatawny soup'
sambar	'liquid, lentil dish eaten with rice'
idli	'rice and lentil cake'
dosa	'pancake made of rice and lentil batter'

These words are from the Dravidian languages, and would have gone into IE specifically from Tamil.

Several words are actually dual sets, particularly culinary items, with one word from English and the other from Hindi at a pan-Indian level.

107.
jeera	cumin
haldi	turmeric
kari patta	curry leaves
amla	gooseberry

Other dual sets are:

108.
reetha	soapnut
dhania	coriander

Compounds from Indian languages also find a place in Indian English:[1]

109.
rail rooko	'agitation in which trains are stopped by protestors'
rasta rooko	'agitation in which roads are blocked by protestors'
jail bharo	'agitation in which jails are filled deliberately by protestors'

It is not easy to distinguish between borrowing and code-switching in these contexts especially because there is no definitive dictionary of Indian English. The same is true, to a lesser degree, of English words in Indian languages. Words like *train, road, car* etc. may be said to be assimilated or borrowed into Indian languages, because there are no equivalent terms. Whether words like *computer*, *PC* and *mouse* are perceived as borrowings into Indian languages cannot be established. Users would be aware that these words belong to a different language.

However, there is no stigma attached to using Indian words in Indian English, unless the words are either taboo words or are informal such as *bindaas* 'brazen' or 'cool'. They would be acceptable in informal speech but not in formal speech or writing.

4.3 Lexical innovations

Since language is a constantly changing phenomenon, it is only to be expected that innovations will take place at various levels. Lexis in IE is no exception to this. The reasons for lexical innovations are many and some of them are quite obvious. English in India is a displaced variety in one sense. New cultures and new needs lead to the creation of several new words that represent the required meanings more adequately. In the case of register – that is, language used for a particular subject – large-scale borrowing happened. The same type of need also leads to the construction of new words today. Local places, things and objects for which terms are absent in English have to be created. Relationships in India need to be more precisely defined.

In formal terms, words are constructed out of two main processes – compounding (in which two or more words are put together to form a single word) and affixation (in which an affix is attached to a word). Additionally, there are a few other processes. All of these are discussed below.

4.3.1 Compounding

Indian languages are rich in compounding and this preference is carried over to IE as well. Several new words have been coined and it is very common to find compounds being constructed instantly. Even in situations where the native English preference is to use a phrase, the Indian preference is to use a compound.

Compounds can be classified according to category as noun-noun (NN) and adjective-noun (AN). As with other varieties of English, NN compounds are the most productive. Some examples of those acceptable in standard Indian English are:

110.
NN

black money	'unaccounted money, earnings on which tax is not paid'
auto-rickshaw	'a motorised three-wheeler'
table fan	'an electric fan meant to be placed on a table'
ceiling fan	'an electric fan meant to be fixed to the ceiling'
pedestal fan	'an electric fan mounted on a tall pedestal'
plate meal	' a meal with fixed portions of various items'
sacred thread	'strands of thread worn by Hindu men, with religious significance'
outstation cheque	'a cheque meant for a recipient who lives in a place away from the issuer of the cheque'
hill station	'a place in the hills which is generally cool in climate'
pass percentage	'the percentage of students who have passed'

god-woman	'a woman who claims spiritual attainment, and the ability to perform miracles'
soapnut	'a herbal extract used for washing hair'
blouse-piece	'a piece of cloth cut to size and sold specifically for getting a blouse stitched'
kitty party	'a women's club of sorts, which meets regularly'

And:

111.

AN
tall claim	'an exaggerated claim'
joining report	'a report given by a person who has joined duty, either at the beginning of employment or after long leave'
creamy layer	'the economically well-off sections of those who belong to underprivileged castes'
gazetted officer	'a government official of a particular rank'
gazetted holiday	'officially notified government holiday'

Some compounds are used as nouns as well as transitive (noun-verb) compounds:

112.

NV
charge-sheet	'an internal list of accusations', 'to conduct an inquiry based on the list of accusations'
double-fry	'an omelette fried on both sides', 'to fry an egg on both sides'

The following are compound verbs:

113.
steam-cook	'to steam food'
air-dash	'to rush by air'

Compounds in which the relationship between the elements is expressed at the sentence level using *for* and *of* are seen in Indian English. Native varieties prefer constructions that combine the two elements with *for*. An oft-quoted example is *match box* which is common in Indian English whereas native varieties would use a *box of matches*. In Indian English it means a box containing matches as well as a box for matches. Similarly, *beer bottle* is a bottle for beer as well as a bottle of beer. *Milk bottle* and *gas cylinder* are other examples. Other compounds for which the native variety preference is to use an *of* phrase are: *chalk piece*, 'piece of chalk'; *key-bunch*, 'bunch of keys'; *meeting notice* 'notice of a meeting' (Yadurajan 2001: 88–9; Trudgill and Hannah 2002: 131). Compounds of this type are very freely constructed in IE and they are acceptable in standard IE.

Another type of compound constructed in Indian English is the *family member* type. Native varieties of English permit compounds in which the head (the word on the right in these compounds) has some recognition in the community. Thus *bus driver* and *school teacher* are permitted in native varieties of English. In Indian English such constructions as *board member, committee member* are also constructed and used freely,[2] including in the standard variety (Yadurajan 2001: 89–90).

Parasher (1983: 29) however notes, in his acceptability study that consisted of two native speakers each of British and American English and two university-level Indian teachers of English, that it was the native speakers who found N + N constructions like *family members, staff members* acceptable. The Indian informants preferred *members of the family, members of the staff* etc. On this basis, he argues that Indian usage and sense of acceptability can be somewhat dated.

Many NN compounds are constructed with a verbal derivative.

114.
playback singer/artiste	'singer who sings for actors in films'
eve-teaser	'male who teases a girl'
room cooler	'electric device which blows cool air'
solar cooker	'cooker powered by solar energy'
milk boiler	'double-walled vessel for boiling milk using steam'
speed breaker	'bump on the road to control speeding'
car-lifter	'car-thief'
child lifter	'kidnapper of children'
stone-pelting	'throwing stones by a mob by way of protest'
eve-teasing	'the act of teasing a girl'
booth capturing	'rigging elections by capturing polling booths'

Below are some compounds that are used adjectivally:

115.
hydro-powered	'powered by hydroelectricity'
self-proclaimed	'proclaimed by oneself'

convent-educated	'denoting one who has studied in a convent school'
Bombay-based	'denoting one based in Bombay'

As Dubey (1994) notes, the most productive forms are those that use the suffixes *-ing* and *-ed*.

Not all the new words constructed are acceptable in standard IE. Words such as those given below would not be acceptable in standard IE.

116.
cousin-sister	'a female cousin'
cousin-brother	'a male cousin'
foreign-returned	'one who has returned after study or work abroad'
native place	'place of birth'
pin-drop silence	'absolute silence'
military hotel	'a non-vegetarian restaurant'

Some of these are region specific but they would not be used in standard writing or speech.

Items like *arranged marriage* and *love marriage* were frowned upon until recently in the education system. The majority of Indian speakers use most of these words freely in their speech without too much concern about the acceptability or standardness. The process of language change is making the non-standard words standard as the free use of *arranged marriage* and *love marriage* shows. Again, as in the case of phonology and syntax, the degree to which non-standard expressions occur in the speech of an individual is unpredictable. Some compounds whose acceptability in standard IE is debatable are:

117.
NN
headbath	'washing one's hair'
pant-piece	'a trouser length'
lemon-set	'a plastic set of jug and glasses to serve juice'

118.
AN
half-pants	'shorts'
English-educated	'one educated in England or in English'
cool drink	'soft drink', 'juice'

4.3.2 Hybrid constructions

Just as there is code-switching at the sentence level which was discussed in the previous chapter, there is code-switching at the word level as well. These have been called hybrid constructions and have been noted in the earliest dictionaries also. Some examples from *Hobson-Jobson* are *swamy house* 'temple to an idol' and *competition-wallah* 'member of the civil service who entered it by the competitive system'.

Again, compounds are the commonest forms among hybrid items. Compounds in which an Indian word is combined with an English word have enabled the expansion of vocabulary in Indian English. A detailed analysis of hybrid constructions is seen in Kachru (1975). Some examples of an Indian word in the modifier or left position are:

119.
ghat road	'a road through the hills or mountains'
gobar gas	'gas formed from cow dung'
Hindipop/Indipop	'fusion of Hindi and popular western music'
iftaar party	'party breaking the fast during Ramadan, in the evening'
kirana store	'grocery store'
baba suit	'adult's dress in reduced form to be worn by little boys'
lathi charge	'caning of demonstrators by police'

Some examples of an Indian word in the head or right position are:

120.
disco bhangra	'a Punjabi dance to disco music'
disco dandia	'a Gujarati dance to disco music'
mutton do-piaza	'a dish of lamb with onions'

4.3.3 Affixation

Affixation is certainly not as productive as compounding. Some prefixes and suffixes appear a little more frequently than others. Some examples given below are sporadic instances of affixation. One of the more frequently used combinations is with *mega* – *mega bonanza, mega sale* etc. This is used to express something that seems great. Another item used in combination like this with a similar meaning is *super-* in the sense of 'great' or 'extraordinary' – *superhit, superstar,* even *super-duper hit* etc.

People hailing from different places are described using certain affixes such as -*ite*.

121.
Delhiite	'one who lives in or hails from Delhi'
UPite	'one who hails from Uttar Pradesh in north India'
hostelite	'inmate of a hostel'
ashramite	'one who lives in an ashram'
Keralite	'one who hails from Kerala in south India'
Naxalite	'refers to Communist extremists, originally meant those who came from Naxalbari in West Bengal where the extremist movement started'

Some place names take English suffixes as follows:

122.
Assamese	'one who hails from Assam'
Maharashtrian	'one who hails from Maharashtra'
Calcuttan	'one who hails from Calcutta'
Tamilian	'one who hails from Tamil Nadu', 'one who speaks Tamil'

The English -*er* as in *Londoner*, *New Yorker* is absent for Indian names. More commonly, an Indian affixed form is used. For example, -*i* indicates that a person comes from that part of the country or indicates the speaker of that language – *Madrasi*,[3] *Bengali*, *Malayali*. These forms are quite perfectly acceptable in standard IE as well. So, a sentence like *He is a Hyderabadi – what does he know of our difficulties?* is standard IE.

There are several hybrid complex words – that is, words in which the affix comes from English. Words like *Brahmoism, Brahminism, Gandhian, Gandhism, Vaishnavism* and *Saivite* are found in native varieites of English as well. It is words like the following that are seen exclusively in IE:

123.
goondaism	'unlawful activities involving violence'
filmi	'artificial', 'melodramatic'

A very common suffix is -*wala* which is used to describe a person associated with a particular activity.

124.
vegetablewala	'vegetable vendor'
paperwala	'newspaper and magazine vendor'
presswala	'journalist'

Many more examples of hybrid names are available in D'souza (2001) which surveys the penetration of English into the Indian milieu and languages.

Other words that are constructed in IE by a process of affixation are given below:

> 125.
> delink   'to separate one unit from another'
> wheatish   'light brown complexion'
> reservationist   'one who espouses the cause of reserving seats in educational institutions and government jobs for certain underprivileged groups'
> derecognise   'to withdraw official recognition, particularly of an institution'

The need for further research is indicated by the word *prepone*. It is generally believed that *prepone* is an IE construction modelled on *postpone* and meaning 'to bring something forward to a time or date earlier than was originally planned'. However, the OED points out that, although in later use it has become common in Indian English, it is in fact also used by native speakers.

4.3.4 Abbreviations, clippings and acronyms

These are plentiful in India. To some extent, generification is also seen. Examples of abbreviations are:

> 126.
> PT   physical training
> AC   air-conditioner
> NRI   Non-Resident Indian
> BSF   Border Security Force
> OBC   Other Backward Castes

The names of institutions and even people are abbreviated:

> 127.
> ANR   Akkineni Nageswara Rao
> NTR   N. T. Rama Rao
> MGR   M. G. Ramachandran
> ICSSR   Indian Council for Social Science Research

ICCR	Indian Council for Cultural Relations
BSNL	Bharat Sanchar Nigam Limited
BHU	Benaras Hindu Univeristy
HCU	Hyderabad Central University
DD	Doordarshan
T.A.	travelling allowance
D.A.	dearness allowance
Non-veg	non-vegetarian

Two examples of acronyms are:

128.
CIEFL /siːɪfəl/	Central Institute of English and Foreign Languages
NABARD	National Bank for Agriculture and Rural Development

And two examples of clippings:

129.
Maths	mathematics
hydel	hydroelectric

Generification:

130.
Godrej	'a steel cupboard'	(originally brought in by Godrej)
Maggi	'instant noodles'	(Maggi being the first brand)

Other indeterminate novel constructions are:

131.
mixie	'a food processor, a machine that mixes food items'
would-be	'fiancé', 'fiancée'
brought-up	'upbringing'
co-brother (in-law)	'one's wife's sister's husband'
co-sister (in-law)	'one's husband's brother's wife'

Other than *mixie*, the rest in (131) are non-standard.

4.3.5 Redundancy

Indian English also tends to use redundant expressions, in which one of the words is usually unnecessary, as in the following words:

132.
potluck lunch
tissue paper
compound word

Here the words *lunch, paper* and *word* are unnecessary. Further examples of using words that are really not required occur when newspapers and magazines are referred to – *Hindu paper, Outlook magazine* and so on. In phrases like *spicy hot* and *chillie hot*, the modifiers are used to remove the ambiguity of the word *hot*.

Another phenomenon by way of redundancy is the loss of the meaning of *re-* in words like *reinstate, rewind* and other words, which are used in sentences with *back* as in:

133.

(a) Rewinding back, how did you start your career as a singer?

(b) They demanded that the ashram reinstate the workers back into service.

(D'souza 2001: 156)

Some more examples:

134.

(a) I will return back home.

(b) I will return your book back.

IE is an interesting combination of items that are obsolete or rare in native varieties of English and those items that are very recent and would be considered colloquial in native varieties. For example, *cod-piece* is used in IE in the sense of 'loincloth'. At the same time words like *majorly* (in all its senses) or *cool* (in the sense of fashionable), which are relatively recent and colloquial, have already found their way into IE. An example of older usage is *dickey* which meant 'a seat in the back of a carriage for servants' in earlier BE. It is now used with the modified meaning in IE of 'a boot of a car'. The extent to which some of the words in IE are relics of earlier BE or are innovations needs to be examined in great detail.

4.4 Discourse features and other strategies of communication

4.4.1 Linkers

Valentine (1991) notes several discourse features in a group of Hindi-English bilingual women speakers. The most common linker in her data is seen to be *and*. The other linkers are *but, or, so, then, well, you know, now, I mean, because* etc. These are conversational markers that bring unity and cohesiveness to speech.

> 135. So I left Delhi when I was ten years old and then I spent uh most of my time in Calcutta – my schooling, and also my graduation. And for my post-graduation when I decided to come back to Delhi, I found out that Delhi has changed a lot... But Calcutta was the place I grew up, and especially for a boy, who's eleven-twelve years old, right up to his graduation...

The above is an extract from an audio recording accompanying this volume. We can clearly see the use of *and* as a linker, even where there is no particular reason to use it.

Gumperz et al. (1982) say that the use of conjunctions in IE discourse differs substantially from Western discourse. Conjunctions in general are said to be optional in Indian languages, therefore such use in IE carries significance.

> B: So so what was the outcome Mr. A?
>
> A: Outcome was that they they had recommended that he has class discipline problem/language problem/so much problem/ and but his lesson was well prepared / and he had told us he needs more help...
> (Gumperz et al. 1982: 45)

In the above example, a significant contrast is brought in by 'but his lesson was well prepared', which is introduced by 'and', but the authors say there is nothing in the tone of voice of the speaker to signal it. They also note that the conjunctions *and* and *but* and the words *yes* and *no* may simply indicate that the speaker wants to say something more.

Very common discourse features heard in India are *I mean, What I mean to say is* and *the thing is*, which are genuinely meant to clarify and are also used as fillers. Valentine (1991) notes the use of *like* which the younger generation uses quite a bit.

4.4.2 Address forms

A striking feature of Indian English discourse appears in its address forms. Relationships in India are rather more clearly defined than in Western societies. Therefore, more precise definitions than *cousin* or *brother-in-law* are required for this society as we saw above. However, the matter does not end there. It is considered disrespectful by this society to address older people by their names. So, all those who are considered to belong to a generation older than oneself are addressed as *aunty* or *uncle*. Thus even to say *Mrs Mamta* or *Mr Raghav* is not acceptable in such a context. A younger person is expected to say *Mamta aunty* or *Raghav uncle*.[4] This is fictive kinship which is required in a society where relationships need to be established (D'souza 1988, Parasher 1999a) and is a direct transfer of what happens when one uses Indian languages.

Children are not allowed to use the names of older people directly and so this mode is expected when they are referring to or addressing older people, such as their friends' parents. In many families, even the servants who are older must be addressed by children as *aunty* or *uncle*. Thus *Jaya aunty* will be used if the maid's name is *Jaya*. If the name is not known or if using the name is considered to be entirely inappropriate by the family, such expressions as *driver uncle* are used. This use of *uncle* and *aunty* is more apparent for fictive relationships than for real ones. Indian words are used for real relationships: *Shekhar-maamaa* /maːmaː/ 'Shekhar (maternal) uncle' or *Vinod-caacaa* /tʃaːtʃaː/ 'Vinod (paternal) uncle'. As is evident, the use of Indian terms becomes necessary because there are different terms for one's relations on the maternal and paternal sides of the family. Indian terms for 'mother' and 'father' are rapidly being replaced by the English *mummy* and *daddy* by the younger generation. Irrespective of the speaker's proficiency in English, this is a curious phenomenon that one sees across the country.

When a person is a little older than oneself, Indian words such as the Hindi *didi* 'elder sister' or *bhai* 'brother (younger or elder)' are used. Since English does not have perfectly synonymous equivalents, the Indian words are used in IE. So, one is likely to hear sentences such as: *Ramesh-bhai told me so; Deepa-didi will bring the books*. Hindi words tend to be used in a cosmopolitan area. In the south, where Hindi is not that well known, Tamil or Telugu equivalents such as *akka* 'elder sister' and *anna* 'elder brother' are used: '*I wanted to buy it, Meena-akka, but Suresh-anna said he would get it for me.*' In case of doubt, no address form is used in conversation.

A woman is not expected to use her husband's name at all. There are other expressions and some circumlocutory ways by which a woman refers to her husband in Indian languages (for this and more on no-naming, see D'souza 1988). In urban areas and among those with an English education, women have begun to use their husband's names and use the expression *my husband*. However, in Indian English it is not uncommon to hear just *he* used by a woman when she is referring to her husband. The context has to determine for the hearer whom she means. This aspect is related to the social class and background of the speaker.

The obverse is not so common. Yet there are societies that do not permit a man to refer to his wife by her name. Even to say *my wife* is considered inappropriate. So, *family* is used by speakers of non-standard English for 'wife'. This is a literal translation, at least in one dialect of Tamil, of the word *samsaaram* /samsa:ram/ which means 'wife' and 'family' among other things. Alternately, *Mrs* is used: *My Mrs is not well today*.

Obviously, this applies to relationships that are at the personal level. At the professional level, the use of *sir* or *madam/ma'am* is expected for one's superiors. This feature has become acceptable in standard IE as well. Addressing a senior person directly – for example, *Professor Jagannath* said by a junior lecturer – is rare. Either *sir* is used or no address form at all. It is when two people are equals that they may be addressed with the titles *Mr, Mrs, Ms, Dr*. Medical doctors and nurses are addressed as *doctor* and *sister* without the use of names. However, when talking in Indian languages, an honorific suffix -*ji*, from Hindi, or its equivalent in other languages, is used. This is transferred to Indian English as well, as in, *Doctor-ji said that he would be fine*. Similarly, when addressing a person in conversation, it is quite acceptable to say *You are right, of course, Shankar-ji* (noted also in Parasher 1999a). Also, children (or even older students) refer to their teachers using either the subject they teach or their names – *economics sir, maths sir, Hindi miss, Physics ma'am, Usha ma'am* or *Abida miss* etc.

A related issue in conversation is that, when talking to a senior person, the use of *you* is avoided since that too is considered to be disrespectful. Students tend to say *As ma'am said*... even while talking to the teacher concerned directly. This, however, is seen only in somewhat non-standard speech and is related to the cultural background of the individual who is speaking.

4.4.3 Welcoming and goodbyes

It is customary in Indian languages to welcome people visiting their places by actually using words that are equivalent to *come*. This feature is transferred to Indian English as well. People are welcomed with *come* or *come, come*. The use of *hello* is seen among equals but is not used for one's superiors or for those older than oneself. Usually, when the relationship is very formal, the Indian *namaste* or *namasteji* is said. The use of *hello* is possible with one's teachers, for example, with the mandatory *sir* or *ma'am*, as in *Hello, ma'am*.

Leave-taking is a prolonged affair. The goodbyes extend over several minutes. This can also be seen on TV news channels where the reporters repeatedly say *thank you* to end a programme. An example is the end of an interview:

> 136.
> Interviewer: Thanks so much.
> Interviewee: Thank you.
> Interviewer: Thanks.

4.5 Aspects of politeness

Politeness takes several forms in speech and writing. One of them is the use of an indirect style in writing and in speech. Euphemisms are preferred to direct expressions – *passed away* is used rather than *die*. Alternately, a higher word like *expired* is used or the sentence *S/he is no more* is used. Similarly, *She is in the family way* or *She is expecting* are preferred over simply saying *She is pregnant*.

D'souza (1988) notes the use of *just* as a marker of a polite request in Indian English. In an utterance like *Just one question*, *just* could either mean 'only' or could actually mean 'please'. In an utterance like *Just move a little* it is a politeness marker. *Would you just move a little* is even more polite. *Please, thank you*, and *sorry* generally do not exist in Indian languages and are usually not used within families.[5] This use of *just* is extremely common and is completely acceptable in standard IE as well.

The tag *no* often stands for *please*. The invariant tag discussed in the preceding chapter is not simply one that stands in for the tags in standard English. It also carries other meanings. In *You have the book, no?*, it is a regular question. But requests like *Come, no* and *Eat, no* are actually pleading and *no* means 'please'. This use of *no* is probably an extension of the Indian language phenomenon. This use is non-standard but users of standard IE would make use of this tag in informal contexts. It is never used in a formal context unless the speaker normally speaks a non-standard variety.

Bhatt (2004) notes that the invariant tag *isn't it?* of non-standard IE (discussed in Chapter 3) serves a similar function. It is a form of unassertiveness and mitigation.

137.

(a) You said you'll do the job, isn't it?

(b) They said they will be here, isn't it?

(Bhatt 2004: 1022)

Examples (137a, b) would be used in non-standard speech and are unassertive.

138.

(a) You said you'll do the job, didn't you?

(b) They said they will be here, didn't they?

(Bhatt 2004: 1022)

However, examples (138a, b) would be used in standard IE and are assertive/intensified.

139.

(a) *Of course you said you'll do the job, isn't it?

(b) *Of course they said they will be here, isn't it?

(Bhatt 2004: 1022)

Thus, in non-standard IE, examples (139a, b) are unacceptable. It is possible that, since the tag serves as a politeness marker, there is no need for a further politeness marker in requests of the following kind:

140.

(a) *Please bring the book, isn't it?

(b) *Shut the door, isn't it?

Interestingly though, the tag *no* can be used in these contexts as well:

141.

(a) Please bring the book, no?

(b) Shut the door, no?

These are acceptable even though they are requests. *No* here is not a genuine question but adds to the politeness of the utterance. This tag sometimes has an element of exasperation and persuasion associated with it depending on the context and is a translation of a Hindi expression that has now spread all over India (Sanyal 2006: 192–3). The tone of voice indicates whether it is politeness or exasperation.

Bhatt (2004) also comments on the use of modals in IE:

142.

(a) This furniture may be removed tomorrow.

(b) These mistakes may please be corrected.

Examples (142a, b) are politer versions of standard IE sentences:

143.

(a) This furniture is to be removed tomorrow.

(b) These mistakes should be corrected.

The question *What's your good name?*, which is a polite way of asking 'What is your name?', is often listed as a pan-Indian one. This is, in fact, used mostly by the speakers of Indo-Aryan languages and is a literal translation of the question that is used in their native languages. It is still a non-standard expression gradually percolating to the speakers of Dravidian languages as well. Yadurajan (2001) notes it as now being a pan-Indian feature.

As with lexical redundancy, there is syntactic circumlocution or indirect expression as well in IE. This is considered to be a typical feature of IE. The use of such expressions is also considered to enhance the politeness of a piece of writing. Some examples are:

144.

(a) I would like to request you to consider my appeal favourably.

(b) I am to invite your attention to the attached invitation.

There are other expressions that are typical of a culture such as India's.

145.

(a) God bless you.

(b) May God bless you.

These are quite acceptable and are used by elders in blessing younger people. In the previous chapter we noted the use of idioms in IE that are literal translations of Indian idioms. In a similar fashion, there are also compliments and blessings such as:

146.
  (a) May you *have many sons* and may you always *wear red.*
  (b) May you *live in your husband's shadow* for a hundred years.

These utterances, taken from Rama Mehta's novel *Inside the Haveli*, are cited by Patil (1999: 52). However, while it would not be correct to say that these are common to everyday use, in circumstances where IE is used as a link language, similar structures like these would be used to bestow blessings. Only someone familiar with the cultural background would recognise the translations and, also to a large extent, the significance of the utterances which indicate that the women should have several sons and must not be widowed, red being the colour for married women in some parts of the country.

4.6 Code-switching with Indian languages

Code-switching also happens at the discourse level as may be expected. A person may change between two or even three languages within a speech act. Such change in language is necessitated by the lack of appropriate vocabulary or other expressions in Indian languages. For example, when talking to one's father or mother, it is possible to express love with the English *I love you, papa* or *I love you, mama*. It is almost impossible to express love in this fashion in Indian languages without sounding ludicrous.

Switching from one language to another also happens because the topic under discussion belongs to a domain that is better suited to a particular language. For instance, the following conversation between two members of a family shows that the subject matter necessitated the switch.

147. Reepu tappakundaa vellaali. We must check the title deeds tomorrow. Monday is the last day for the discounted offer. Pillalu een ceestaaru? Ontari-gaa untaaree!	'We must go tomorrow. We must check the title deeds tomorrow. Monday is the last day for the discounted offer. What will the children do? They will be all by themselves!'

Another reason that necessitates a switch is a change in strategy from the point of view of the speaker.

148. This is inconvenient for me.   'This is inconvenient for me.
    Miiru oka saari naato   If you had told me over the
    phone-loo ceppeestee, naaku   phone once, I would not have had
    ii srama undeedi kaadu.   to go through this trouble'.

The change from English to Telugu in the above piece is by way of softening the implied censure in the English sentence. English, as stated in the first chapter, increases distance, whereas one's own language closes it.

However, Singh (1995) rightly points out that the matter is not quite as simple as that. Whether English is used as the nearness language or as the distancing language depends on the relationship between the speakers and the audience involved. English may actually be used as the language that establishes closeness rather than distance as is shown in the conversation below:

149. A: Tell Archna not to make that much noise, aur aap bhi Rekha se mana kar dijiye ('and you should tell Rekha the same').

(Singh 1995: 132)

A is speaking to his wife and his cousin. While his wife is public-school educated, his cousin comes from the country. In this case, clearly, English is used as the nearness language and Hindi is actually used as the distancing language. The educated classes often believe that English is their language.

Parasher (1999a: 27) gives the following example of code-switching that is used to reiterate a message:

150. Please do sit down, beithiye sahib.

Here the Hindi is a repetition of the English expression. Note that politeness is further enhanced by the use of both *please* and *do*.
Code-switching is also used to qualify a message:

151. Just wait, we're leaving in a few minutes, nehin to gaadi chut jayegi. ('or else we'll miss the train').

(Parasher 1999a: 27)

There are thus several reasons for code-switching. Most often a switch in language happens merely because the two speakers are comfortable in both languages. An extended conversation often happens in two languages. This is increasingly evident in Indian films, especially Hindi ones, without the mandatory translations that used to exist in earlier films.

4.7 Style

The style of IE has been said to be archaic and formal. In Chapter 3 it was noted that there is an overall preference for the use of Romance words – that is words of Latinate origin. There are also several constructions that are unacceptable to native speakers of English in terms of appropriateness (Parasher 1983). Letters that contain structures such as the following are quite common in IE:

152.

  (a) Respected Madam...

  (b) This has reference to your letter...

  (c) Kindly do the needful.

  (d) We shall be highly obliged to you...

  (e) We request you to please recommend...

  (f) I shall be thankful if you would...

  (g) Please arrange to do this at your earliest convenience...

  (h) Thanking you in advance...

  (i) Thanking you for your kind consideration...

  (j) Yours most obediently...

Native speakers tend to use more direct constructions and avoid circumlocutory utterances. Many of the constructions in (152) above occur in the writing of users of standard IE as well.

It is also quite common to hear proficient speakers of Indian English changing their manner of speech depending on the context. So, in an informal context, the same speaker will use structures which s/he will not use in more formal situations.

153.

	Informal	Formal
(a)	Do like this.	Do it this way.
(b)	This is correct, no?	This is correct, isn't it?
(c)	This is OK, na?	This is OK, isn't it?

These different forms are chosen according to the context. Just as careful speech makes for more 'correct' grammar and a more polished accent, lexis and discourse features also become more formal or standard.

Notes

1. The words *rail* and *jail* are assimilated into Indian languages – the former means 'train' in India.
2. There are reasons to believe that these are compounds and not syntactic constructions. To give just one piece of evidence, *new board member* can only mean 'a new member of the board' and not 'a member of a new board'.
3. The word *Madrasi* is used in North India to refer to all South Indians and also has a pejorative connotation.
4. It will be observed that it is not Aunt(y) Mamta or Uncle Raghav. The sequence in which the kinship terms appear in Indian languages is reproduced in Indian English.
5. Hindi has words equal to *thank you* that are used in everyday conversation as well. Other languages also have equivalents but the words are too formal for everyday interaction. In modern times, *thank you* and *thanks* are used by bilinguals even if they are conversing in an Indian language. The same is true of *please* and *sorry*.

5 History and Changes in Progress

Thomas Babington Macaulay's historic 'Minute' on Indian Education of 2 February 1835 is generally perceived to be the starting point of English education in India. While this is correct, it is true in a particular sense. Macaulay's 'Minute' was instrumental in establishing English as the medium of instruction in educational institutions of higher learning. But, even prior to this institutionalisation, there were attempts at English education in India by several independent and other organisations. The first serious forays into India by Englishmen began with the establishment of the East India Company by the granting of a charter by Queen Elizabeth I, to a few merchants of the City of London, giving them monopoly of trade with the East, on 31 December 1600. By 1611, British factories began to be established in different coastal places in India. Over two centuries of contact with the British was obviously going to have an impact on the language situation of the country. The events relating to language cannot be divorced from the politico-historical, cultural and religious factors that shape a nation. This chapter will trace some of the significant events that contributed to the establishment of English in India. Since India is a vast, populous country, many areas will perforce be left out of the picture in this short space. The focus will remain on the three Presidencies – Madras, Calcutta and Bombay. It should be remembered that independence in 1947 was accompanied by the vivisection of India into what are now three countries.

While the historical and political factors served to establish English as an important language in the country, this process had linguistic consequences. Style and spelling underwent gradual changes along the line. Besides, languages in contact give rise to new pidgins, which are discussed in this chapter.

5.1 History

5.1.1 The pre-British period (1498–1600)

The British were not the first Europeans to enter the land in the modern period. The Portuguese, the more successful and prosperous traders belonging to a vibrant nation of that time, were. In 1498, Vasco da Gama found a sea route to India, landing on the west coast, in the south at Calicut. He gained trading rights from the local authority, the Zamorin. By 1510, the Portuguese began to exercise political power as well. Alfonso de Albuquerque seized Goa from the Bijapur Sultanate. Goa became the trading nerve centre for the Portuguese. India was a continuum of princely states until the twentieth century. Constant battles and wars kept changing the contours of these states, before and after Europeans began to gain control of territories.

Other Europeans – the Dutch and the English, for example – initially came to India on Portuguese ships. Father Thomas Stephens, who set sail for India from Lisbon on 4 April 1579 and arrived in October of the same year, is considered to be the first Englishman to settle in India.[1] He was a Jesuit priest associated with a staunchly Catholic nation, Portugal. The letters he wrote to his father constitute the first examples of Anglo-Indian literature. His vision was that Englishmen should follow the example of the Portuguese. England far surpassed his expectations!

Portugal had a very clear policy of proselytisation, the trend being set by St Francis Xavier. The processes of acquiring territories and missionary activity continued simultaneously. Portugal gained control along the west coast of the south and also went as far as Hoogly, near Calcutta, on the east coast. They also had establishments at Daman and Diu in modern-day Gujarat. All of these were far away from Delhi, the seat of Moghul power. Issues of polity and the absence of European women led Albuquerque to encourage marriage between the Portuguese and local Indian women. Mass marriages were not unheard of.

The influx of the Portuguese led to language contact between their tongue and the local languages. As a consequence of this, a Portuguese pidgin developed which served as the lingua franca. This variety came to be termed Patois by the Europeans and Firanghee ('foreign') by the Indians (especially in Bengal). This variety was also the language of communication among the Europeans who came to the country due to the formation of trading companies, by the British in 1600, the Dutch in 1602, the Danes in 1616 and the French in 1644. It became necessary for all Europeans to learn Portuguese in order to manage in India. The East India Company had two hundred Portuguese dictionaries and a

Portuguese language expert in every trading factory in India, in the seventeenth century. English itself was confined to their own trade centres. Interpreters became quite common during this time and most of them were Indians. It is recorded that, as the ships approached, local youngsters would rush to the harbours to offer their services as interpreters and earn some money in this fashion.

As a result of these activities, there was substantial exchange of vocabulary across languages. Portuguese words entered English and so did Indian words. Some of the Indian words prevalent in English today came into the language through Portuguese (see Chapter 4).

Goa continued to be the stronghold of the Portuguese even as England gradually gained control of the rest of the nation. When India gained independence from the British in 1947, Pondicherry and Yanam on the east coast were in the control of France and Goa was in the control of Portugal. In 1954, the French vacated their territories peacefully but the Portuguese refused to leave, in spite of appeals from the Indian Government and the international community. In 1961, the Indian army marched its way into Goa and met with little resistance, and Goa became a part of the Indian nation. Thus the Portuguese, who were the first Europeans to come, were the last to leave.

English begins to be a significant language as early as 1676. However, the early English settlers were neither interested in imparting education, nor in missionary activity. The most important contribution of Portuguese for the future introduction of English had already been the Roman script. Before English took over India, the script of the language had already been introduced (Sinha 1978). The very presence of Portuguese implies this. Further, the use of the Roman script was facilitated through the catechisms, which were prepared by them in the Roman script.

5.1.2 The pre-Macaulay period (1600–1835)

These two centuries constitute the period of entry, accession and consolidation of British power in the subcontinent. The British came as traders and their initial efforts were obviously confined to such activities. The first trading post was set up in Surat on the west coast in 1612, after rights were granted by the Moghul emperor Jahangir. After a great deal of humiliation, Sir Thomas Roe managed to procure further trading rights for Britain in India. Subsequently, other places became available to England and several other factories such as the one in Machilipatnam, in the east, came to be established. This was shifted to Madras and this city eventually became a major centre in the south of India. Similarly, in the east, it was Hoogly and in the west, Bombay. Interestingly, Bombay became a British territory when it was given to Britain by Portugal, as dowry for Catherine of Braganza, who married King Charles II in 1662. The city of Calcutta was constructed by the British through the amalgamation of a few villages in the Hoogly delta. Fort St George was built in Madras and Fort William in Calcutta. Slowly but surely, the East India Company gained control of territories across India from Indian rulers and the other colonisers, mostly by means of wars and *Dewanees* (land grants with authority to collect revenue). Commencing with the victory of Lord Robert Clive in the Battle of Plassey in 1757, Moghul rule gradually became subservient to the East India Company. The three major cities where the British established their trading ports became the three major Presidencies of the (later) Raj. Calcutta was the centre that the British governed their territories from, until the capital was changed to Delhi in 1911.

The East India Company kept vacillating between permitting missionaries and prohibiting their activities throughout its rule. With the charter renewal of 1698, missionary activity became possible for the British, through the missionary clause that was inserted, allowing them to come to India to propagate the Protestant religion. This was seen to be necessary when all the other countries were propagating Catholicism and the British could not let it gain ground. While the Ministers were to learn Portuguese, the languages advocated for the local people by the charter were the vernaculars (as the local languages were called then). Initial education was evangelical in nature. In teaching the local people, different languages were tried. 'Malaian' meaning Tamil and/or Malayalam was used. Then, books in Portuguese were used. These attempts were not successful, the latter because Patois was used in India which had only an empirical resemblance to Portuguese as used in Portugal. So, books in 'pure' Portuguese were as unintelligible as English books to the local people (Law 1915).

Secular education became the concern of the East India Company and the missionaries from about 1670. The directors made enquiries about children in Fort St George, and pronounced their views on how they should be brought up. In 1673 a Scot preacher, Pringle, was appointed and he kept a school for British and Portuguese Eurasians and a few children of the Indian subordinates for whom the company felt responsible. The medium of instruction was 'the debased kind of Portuguese' (Law 1915: 12). Several other teachers came after Pringle. Mr Lewis, the company's chaplain at Fort St George (1691–1714), studied Portuguese and imparted religious education in that language. Mr Lewis himself started a free school in the Fort and this was later

Figure 5.1 India 1698

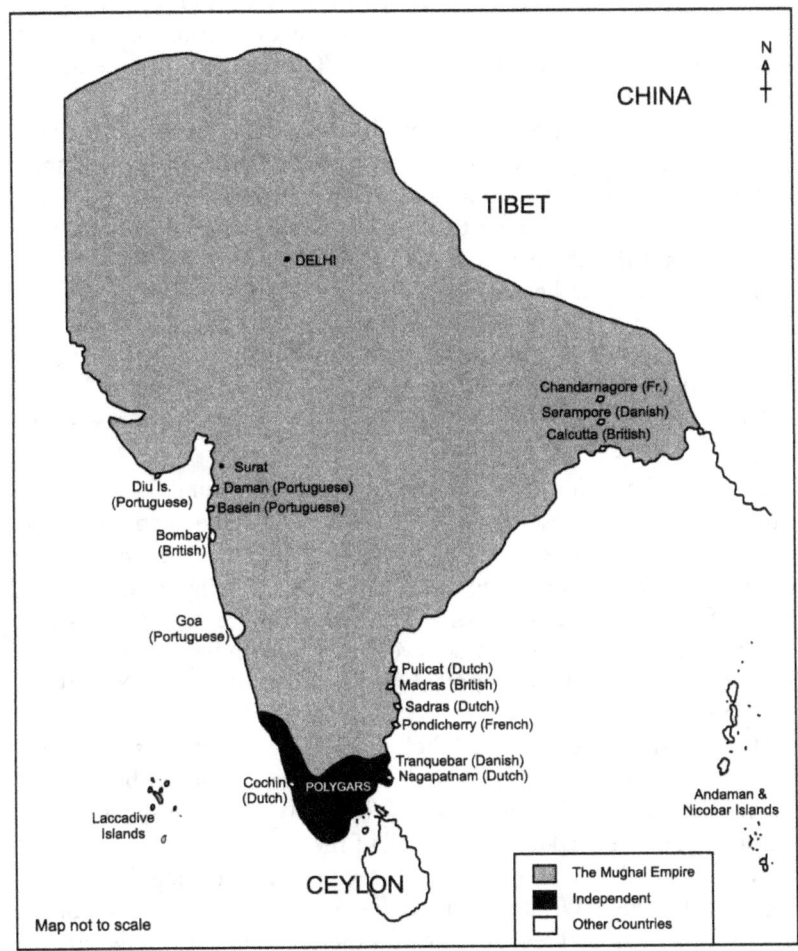

continued by his successor, Rev. William Stevenson. In December 1715, Rev. William Stevenson decided to make the break with Portuguese by starting the first English school in Madras for Eurasians.

This school was the beginning of a series of charity schools set up – one in Bombay in 1719 by Richard Cobbe and one in Calcutta in 1739 by the Society for the Promotion of Christian Knowledge. The Bombay school marked the beginning of the Education Society Schools and the Calcutta school led to the establishment of other schools and the Free School Society. These schools were primarily meant for Protestant children. By the first half of the eighteenth century, English medium schools and the teaching of the Gospel were fairly well established in the three Presidencies. The Society for the Promotion of Christian Knowledge started a circulating library in Calcutta in 1709, the first of its kind in India.

1765 is the most significant date in the history of the East India Company. In this year, the Company acquired a *Deewanee* or a land grant of three regions – Bengal, Bihar and Orissa – from Emperor Shah Alam, who was by then a mere titular head of the Moghul empire. The *Deewanee* gave the company the right to collect revenue in these places. This constitutes the beginning of the rule of East India Company in India. Further territories were acquired gradually by several different means, by the British. For instance, Richard Wellesley's policy of subsidiary alliance weakened Indian States. Under this policy, an allying ruler was to permit the permanent stationing of a British force in the State.

A shift in the policy of the East India Company around the same time brought about an upsurge of emotion among some sections of the British. In the charter renewal this time, the missionary clause was scrapped, thereby prohibiting missionaries from coming to India on the ships of the East India Company. The decision to remove the missionary clause was triggered by a revolt in south India. Obviously, the company did not want to jeopardise its lucrative business for the sake of religion.

The missionaries saw it as their duty to uplift Indians and bring them to the 'light of Christianity'. They were supported by William Wilberforce and Lord Castlereagh. William Wilberforce spoke in parliament on this issue. However, not all of the British concurred with this view and the missionary clause was indeed removed during this Charter renewal. In 1784, William Pitt's India Act was passed by which the company gained joint responsibility for the governance of India with the British Crown. The British Government took this decision partly out of desire to partake of the enormous riches 'John Company' (the East India Company) brought back home and partly out a sense of anxiety about the atrocities that might be committed by unhindered traders.

Interest in India and its education continued irrespective of Government. In the same year as the India Act, Sir William Jones established the Asiatic Society, on 15 January 1784, in Calcutta, as a centre for 'Asian studies including almost everything concerning man and nature within the geographical limits of the continent' (The Asiatic Society 2007). In 1778, the first English printing press was established in Hoogly. The period 1780–95 saw the establishment of several English newspapers in the three Presidencies. 1781 is a significant date in the history of this period, with the establishment of a madrasa (religious teaching establishment) for the Muslims in Calcutta by Warren Hastings. He defrayed the initial costs himself and was later reimbursed by the company and the college was given to the Government. This became an important centre of study for Muslims, who he thought were deprived of education. 1794 is significant for the publication of the first book in English by an Indian. Dean Mahomet wrote an autobiographical account of his life and travels in India and England in the book *The Travels of Dean Mahomet*.

Charles Grant, belonging to the Clapham Sect and a Member of Parliament for many years representing the County of Inverness, was an eminent director of the East India Company. He wrote an extensive treatise in 1792 which he submitted to his colleagues in 1797 pleading that it was the duty of the British to impart Christian education to Indians. The oft-quoted lines from his treatise are:

> The true cure of darkness is the introduction of light. The Hindoos err, because they are ignorant; and their errors have never fairly been laid before them. The communication of our light and knowledge to them, would prove the best remedy for their disorders... (quoted in Mahmood 1981: 11)[2]

Towards the end of the treatise, he summarises his arguments as follows:

> Thus, we trust, it has been evinced, that although many excellent improvements have of late years been made in the Government of our Indian territories, the moral character and condition of the Natives of them is extremely depraved, and that the state of society among that people is, in consequence, wretched ... A remedy has been proposed for these evils;–the introduction of our light and knowledge among that benighted people, especially the pure, salutary, wise principles of our divine religion. (quoted in Mahmood 1981: 15)

His plea was that this knowledge must be imparted in English; this was probably the first serious argument for English in India.

> The first communication, and the instrument of introducing the rest, must be the English language; this is a key which will open to them a world of new ideas, and policy alone might have impelled us, long since, to put it into their hands. (quoted in Mahmood 1981: 12)

In the meantime, as far as English education was concerned, more schools continued to be established, for different purposes. Up to 1787, all educational activities were taken up by the missionaries, in particular

Figure 5.2 India 1798

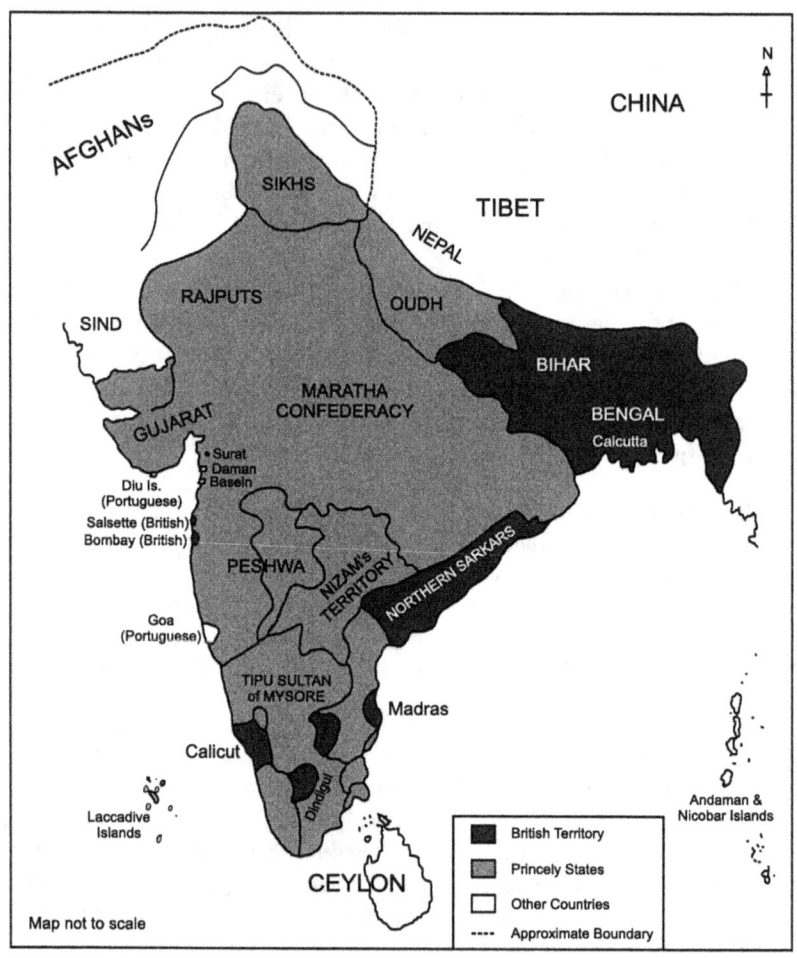

by the Society for the Promotion of Christian Knowledge (Law 1915). The East India Company supported these activities but did not directly participate in them. Charity schools were established at Ramnad and Sivaganga in the south with the help of local rulers, putting aside the charter, in 1785. Other private schools were established by some English people, mostly widows or pensioners who needed to make a living. It was in these schools that Indians had access to English education. These schools counted some well-known figures as their pupils. Dwaraknath Tagore and Raja Ramnath Tagore studied in Mr Sherburn's school in

Calcutta. These private schools indicate the public acceptance of English education. Most of the missionary schools lasted as long their funds lasted. The private ones lasted as long as their founders did (Sinha 1978).

Between 1813 and 1823, during Warren Hastings' stewardship, the British expanded their dominions and Baroda, Travancore, Poona, Hyderabad and Oudh came under British rule. The charter came up for renewal again in 1813 and, this time, Charles Grant argued vociferously for the inclusion of the missionary clause. William Wilberforce told Parliament to 'exchange [India's] dark and bloody superstition for the genial influence of Christian light and truth' (Kachru 1994: 504). The House of Commons decided that it was the duty of Britain to introduce useful knowledge and knowledge of moral upliftment to the natives of British India. All support was to be extended to those who went to India for this purpose and education was brought directly under the control of the East India Company. This was implemented in spite of contrary viewpoints, such as those expressed by Randle Jackson who feared that education would make England lose India just as it had lost its colonies in America. The Charter Act this year included an educational clause allocating one lakh (one hundred thousand) rupees per annum for education. This clause led quickly to the first major language debate in India termed the Anglicist-Orientalist debate. This is also the first official acceptance of British responsibility for the education of Indians. The Court of Directors sent the Governor-General of India the first despatch on educational responsibility, the mandate being thus given to begin educational activities for the local people.

But before this, some colleges were also established. The Banaras Sanskrit College was started in 1791 by Jonathan Duncan and was maintained by the Government almost as a match to the madrasa founded earlier by Warren Hastings in 1781. The main purpose of the colleges was to encourage native learning and provide an economic possibility for the Hindus and Muslims of India. Lord Minto's Minute on Education endorsed this approach and argued that encouragement of native knowledge would cure some of the ills of Indian society. However, the primary function of the two oriental colleges was to provide the British administration with youth who could work for them, especially Hindu and Muslim law officials for judicial administration.

The Hindu College was set up in Calcutta in 1817 due to individual initiatives by Indians and imparted English education. This college was later merged with the Presidency College of Calcutta. The prime movers of this college were David Hare, an uneducated English watchmaker, and Raja Rammohun Roy, a leading light of the Indian

Renaissance. Initially private, the college ran into financial difficulties and requested the government to take it over; it then became the first English college of the government.

In the west, Bombay Presidency was established in 1818 with the overthrow of the Peshwa and Lord Elphinstone became the first Governor. Several colleges were started during this time in the north and the west. The Bombay Native Education Society set up District Schools in the Bombay Presidency, with Elphinstone as the President in 1823, and it contributed considerably to the cause of education during this period. These schools adopted indigenous methods, prepared books in Indian languages and also introduced a few English schools. In his Minute of 13 December 1823, Elphinstone thought it advisable to introduce English education gradually, by starting one school in each district. The Superintendent of the Poona Sanskrit College (started in 1821 for the benefit of destitute Brahmins who had lost their livelihood as a result of British take-over), Captain Candy observed:

> The national education of India cannot be said to be on a suitable basis till there is a vernacular school in every village and an English school in every Zilla. After these have been in operation a few years, I doubt not there will be added to them a college for every province. (Sinha 1978: 47)

Elphinstone and Candy were wary of introducing English education in a hurry. They preferred to admit students to English study only if they were already proficient in their own languages. Moreover, they were not desirous of upsetting the upper classes who were already considerably dispossessed. And finding good teachers to teach English was a difficulty. But Warden, Member of the Governor's Council, was for ensuring universal English education. Sir John Malcolm, who succeeded Elphinstone, was in favour of vernacular education. Thus, Bombay was caught in the Anglicist-Vernacularist conflict. Bombay was in favour of the vernaculars, and was grappling with the problem of how to integrate English into the education system. The Poona Sanskrit college was asked at the instance of Warden, if they would like to introduce English into the curriculum. When this proposal was accepted, the funds allocated to this college were increased. On 21 September 1826, the Court of Directors sent a despatch to the Bombay Presidency appreciating the establishment of an English School.

Similarly, English was introduced as a subject in Agra College and the Calcutta madrasa. But Calcutta had a different debate – on whether English should become the medium of instruction or the classical, oriental languages, Sanskrit and Arabic, should. The Orientalists proposed the nativist theory that argued that the languages that were already in use should continue. Prominent British advocates of this theory were H. T. Prinsep, Houghton Hodgson (who worked for the East India Company) and John Wilson (a missionary scholar). The Anglicists, on the other hand, proposed the transplant theory and voiced the view that a new language could indeed be used to impart education. Prominent among the Anglicists were Charles Grant (1746–1823) and Lord Moira (1754–1826). The Anglicists had supporters from among Indians as well and this debate was certainly not a divide between the East and the West. Raja Rammohun Roy's letter of 11 December 1823 to Lord Amherst is a case in point. While opposing the setting-up of a Sanskrit college in Calcutta, the letter urges the Governor to make available to Indians all that is best in Western education. This letter, in fact, makes no mention of English at all but talks of the uselessness of Sanskrit grammar and Vedanta (Roy 1999). Of the two Presidencies, Bombay had a stronger group of anti-Anglicists. The reason for this lay in the strength of the vernaculars that were both spoken and written, whereas the Oriental (classical) languages were not spoken but were merely the languages of education.

From the administrative point of view, the East India Company saw fit to send despatches to the three Presidencies encouraging them to move to English education. In 1823, the General Committee of Public Instruction was constituted to oversee matters concerning education. In 1830, the Court sent despatches to the Presidencies stating explicitly that it wanted Indians to have access to European sciences and literatures. A more emphatic note was used for Madras clearly indicating that Indians more suited for administrative work would be desirable. Madras drew particular attention because the debate here during the preceding years was not on language but on whether or not to impart Christian knowledge. During 1818–1831, the missionaries were very active, opening many centres. Female education got a boost. The Madras School Book Society requisitioned a report from Vennelacunty Soob Row in 1820 as to the state of affairs with regard to school education of the local people. In this report, Soob Row voices his concern about the state of teaching of Telugu in the Presidency which was mere rote learning. Also, he notes that the manner of English teaching was deficient in that the students were exposed only to a small number of books. Overall, he argues that the quality of English acquired by the local people was not good (Soob Row 1873). The court noted all this but thought that Madras lagged behind.

By now the Anglicist-Orientalist debate was at its peak. Over a period of time, the committee realised the difficulty of teaching science through translation and began to want English as the medium of instruction. The popularity of the Hindu College and the dwindling numbers of students for oriental learning split the committee into equal numbers of Orientalists and Anglicists. The debate on how to use the one lakh rupees took over. In 1835, at this juncture, Lord Thomas Macaulay was made the first Law member of the Council and Head of the Committee of Public Instruction.

5.1.3 The pre-independence period (1835–1947): The institutionalisation of English education

Macaulay's 'Minute' very clearly argues for English as the medium of instruction at higher levels, rather than the Oriental languages. The 'Minute' constitutes an example of colonialist and imperialist attitude of superiority. Macaulay averred that the Oriental languages did not possess any knowledge worth preserving:

> I have conversed, both here and at home, with men distinguished by their proficiency in the Eastern tongues. I am quite ready to take the oriental learning at the valuation of the orientalists themselves. I have never found one among them who could deny that a single shelf of a good European library was worth the whole native literature of India and Arabia. The intrinsic superiority of the Western literature is indeed fully admitted by those members of the committee who support the oriental plan of education...
>
> How then stands the case? We have to educate a people who cannot at present be educated by means of their mother-tongue. We must teach them some foreign language. The claims of our own language it is hardly necessary to recapitulate. It stands pre-eminent even among the languages of the West...
>
> We must at present do our best to form a class who may be interpreters between us and the millions whom we govern, a class of persons Indian in blood and colour, but English in tastes, in opinions, in morals and in intellect.
> (Macaulay 1835)

Raja Rammohun Roy's letter had been passed on by Lord Amherst to the Committee of Public Instruction and it had been put aside by them. The Calcutta Sanskrit College that Roy opposed was founded. The influence of Raja Rammohun Roy's letter is nevertheless evident on Macaulay, in talking of the same matters. In spite of H. T. Prinsep's dissent note (Prinsep 1835), in which he addressed and argued against each point made by Macaulay, the Governor-General, Lord William Bentinck, gave his seal of approval to Macaulay's 'Minute' on 7 March 1835 and English became the language of higher education in India. This continues to be the situation even today, after one and three quarter centuries.

An official resolution endorsing the 'Minute' was passed and, in brief, it recommended the following: to promote European literature and science using all funds for English education alone; not to abolish institutions of native learning but not support students of native learning (with stipends); when a Professor of Oriental learning retired, the decision of appointing a successor was to be determined depending on the number of students etc.; not to utilise funds for printing of oriental works; to use all such released funds for imparting English literature and science in English; and the Committee was to submit to the government a plan for the implementation of these instructions.

In Bombay, Sir Thomas Perry became the President of the Board of Education. Although a staunch Anglicist, he could implement English education only in the face of stiff opposition from the vernacularists on the board.

The period 1844 to about 1905, until the beginning of nationalism, saw a series of policy decisions by the British administration that implemented English education in different ways. This period was also the beginning of the era of Commission Reports. Hardinge, the Governor-General, decided to open subordinate office jobs to Indians. The purpose was to encourage the use of English and provide cost-economic staff to the British. His policy came in for criticism because the teaching of English at this time was too literary and lacked purpose. Nevertheless, since English was taught without reference to religion, a middle-class, English-speaking gentry was created. During this time, Madras tried to have two different types of English classes – one with the Bible and the other without, leaving the option of attending either one to the students. The Marquis of Tweeddale, then Governor of Madras, who proposed this in a minute, thought that eventually many people would be converted to Christianity. The Court of Directors disapproved of this approach and advocated religious non-interference once again. Nevertheless, the advancement of English education in the Madras Presidency was more due to the efforts of the missionaries than those of the authorities.

During the time that Dalhousie was Governor-General, the policy of annexation through the Doctrine of Lapse was implemented. By this, when the ruler of any princely state died without an heir, the state became British. British dominions expanded considerably during this time. This was also a period of considerable development and industrialisation. The railways, postal service and telegraph were introduced. Indians were permitted to sit the examinations for Civil Services. All these events gave rise to a need for English-speaking Indians and English education came to be in great demand. Dalhousie was nevertheless cautious in implementing English education. He saw the need for English but encouraged the vernacular languages. Several educational institutions also came up during this time. A number of engineering, medical and polytechnic institutions were founded. The Bethune School, Calcutta, started in 1849 and, imparting English education, was the first of a number of schools started for girls.

The first major Commission Report on Indian Education was written by a committee under the presidentship of Charles Wood, in 1854. Called the Magna Carta of Indian Education, it made several recommendations, the most important being the establishment of universities. The other major suggestions were that: teacher-training institutes should be set up; the vernaculars and classical languages should be encouraged and taught; English should be used for higher education and the vernaculars taught at lower levels; attention should be shifted to educating the masses; religious neutrality must be maintained; and occupational education must be implemented. The Education Department was instituted as a separate administrative unit.

1857 saw the first War of Independence (or the Sepoy Mutiny, depending on who the historian is), which was ruthlessly crushed. The government went ahead with the setting up of three universities, in the three Presidencies, which showed its confidence in remaining in India for a long enough duration.

The Hunter Commission, officially known as the Indian Education Commission, was set up in 1882 and was presided over by Sir William Wilson Hunter. It included Indians in the committee and submitted its report in October 1883. Its focus was on primary education, for which it made thirty-six recommendations.

The Indian National Congress was formed in 1885 and was instrumental in leading the country to independence. It is interesting to note that, in the circular announcing its first meeting, the prerequisite for a delegate was knowledge of English (Thirumalai 2004). It was believed by some scholars and leaders that English had the effect of unifying Indians across the country and catalysing the nationalistic impulse. Both the English language, which served as a link language, and English education, which was supposed to have sown ideas of liberty, were deemed responsible for the Indian nationalist movement. This view was articulated by Surendra Nath Banerjea and others (McCully 1966), whereas Mohandas Karamchand Gandhi, who returned to India in 1915 from South Africa, was dismissive of it.

In 1904, the Indian Universities Act was passed and it heralded the setting-up of a number of universities. Immediately after this, in 1905,

Figure 5.3 India 1857

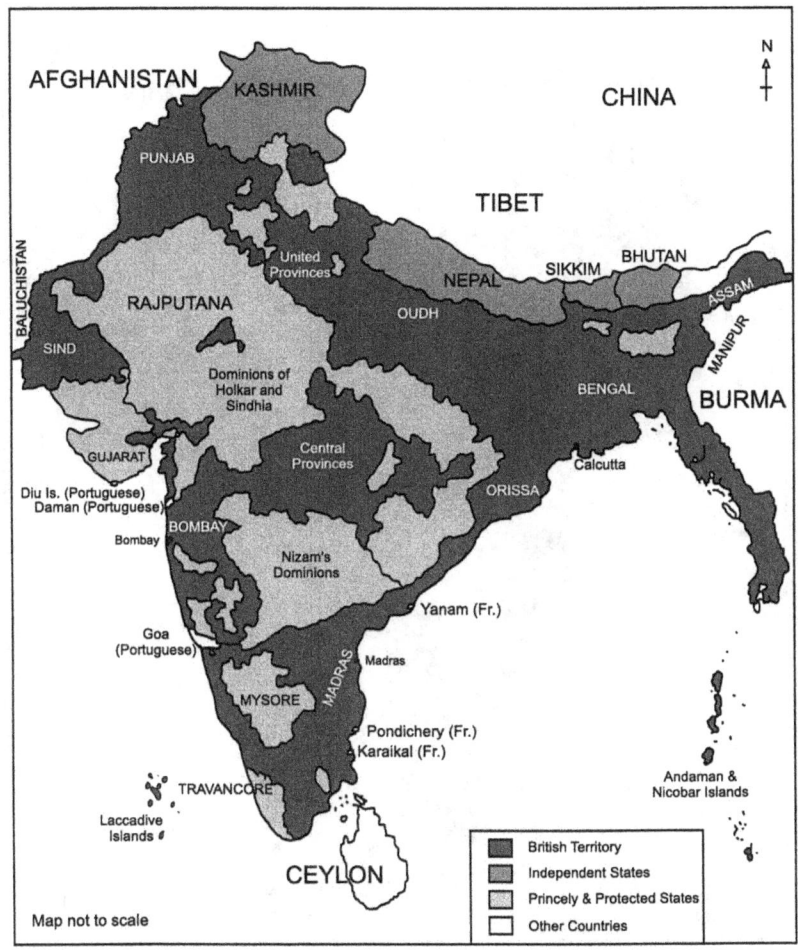

came the partition of Bengal. This event led to nationalistic fervour, yet English was not rejected.

Later, control of the education departments was transferred, first to the provinces, and, from 1921 onwards, to Indians. The issues concerning education were deliberated upon by several committees.

However, a major issue during this period, in anticipation of independence, was what the national language of the country was to be. Indian national leaders met in Calcutta at a conference in 1916 and advocated the use of Hindustani as the national language of India. Those

Figure 5.4 India 1935

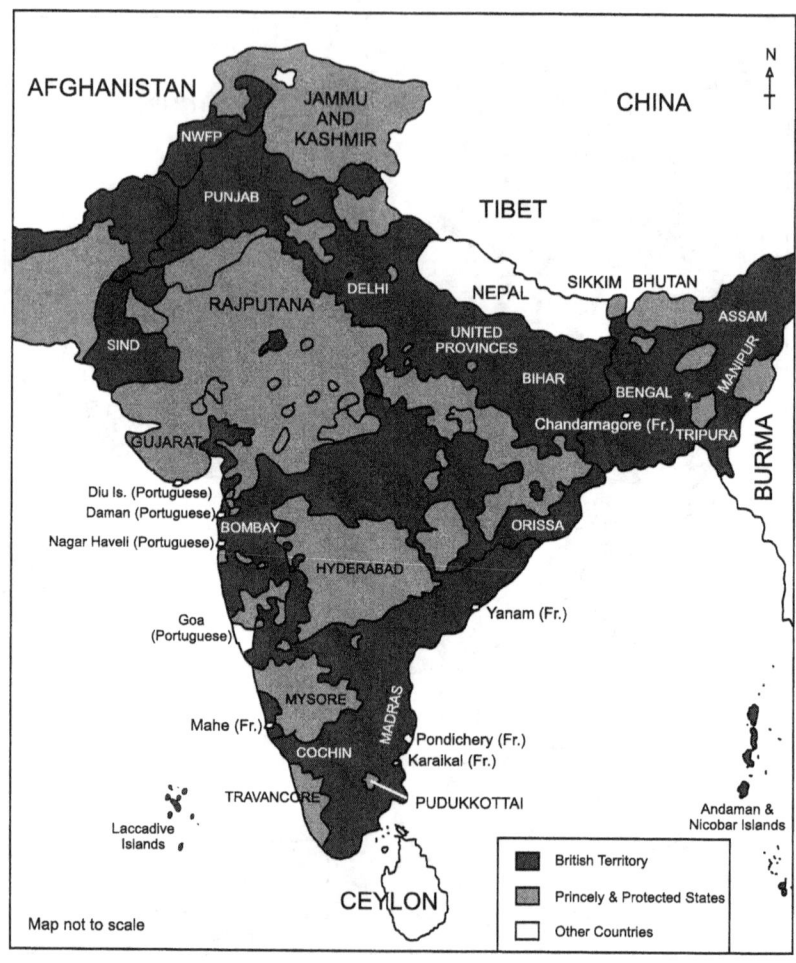

such as Gandhi, Bal Gangadhar Tilak, Pandit Madan Mohan Malaviya, Maulana Mohammed Ali and Maulana Abul Kalam Azad were a part of this resolution (Chib 1936: 8).

5.1.4 The post-independence period (1947–2006)

Around the time of independence, language debates raged which were simply a continuation of the debates that the national leaders were exercised about. Four languages or dialects were contenders for the position of national language: Sanskrit, Hindi, Hindustani and English. Sanskrit and Hindi were advocated by those who were elitist in one form or another. Sanskrit being the language of ancient Hindu knowledge and Hindi, with its Sanskrit vocabulary, were used by the upper classes. Both M. K. Gandhi and Jawaharlal Nehru preferred the use of Hindustani, which was colloquial and closer to the people, but for different reasons (Sonntag 2000). In truth, Nehru was a votary of a modern and scientifically advanced India and his personal preference was for English. But, because it was not long after the end of foreign rule, Nehru and others did not argue strongly in favour of English. Gandhi, with his views of village economy, advocated the use of Hindustani, which he saw also as a unifying language between the Hindus and Muslims.

The serious opposition of the south and Bengal to either Hindi or Hindustani led to a situation in which no language was chosen to be the national language of the country. Up to 1950, when India became a republic and the Constitution was adopted, the country was governed by the Central Legislative Assembly, which also doubled as the Constituent Assembly that framed the Constitution. In the Constituent Assembly, the discussion of the language of the Union took place and its members were equally divided on the language issue as to whether Hindi or English was to be the official language of the country. The President of the Assembly, Dr Rajendra Prasad (later, President of India) exercised his casting vote in favour of Hindi.

Thus it was that Hindi became the official language of the country. However, English was retained as an official language for all the purposes that it was used for until independence, for a period of fifteen years from the adoption of the Constitution up to 1965. During this time, Hindi was to gradually replace English in all contexts. Most people think that Hindi is the national language of India and this myth has been continuously perpetrated. In fact, it was meant to be, and remains, an official language.

The status of English as 'associate' official language came up for review before 1965. People in the south, much agitated over the issue, rioted. In the meantime, trouble brewed within the south itself. The Madras State was vast, with people of different language groups residing in it. There was a strong perception among the non-Tamilians that all developmental activities were confined to the Tamil-speaking areas. The Telugus, in particular, agitated for a separate state. The Telugu bid for separate governance was not new – it had begun in the 1930s. Finally, in 1955, the linguistic reorganisation of states was ordered by the government, after the death by fasting of Potti Sriramulu in 1952.

These language riots were soon followed by the anti-Hindi riots in Tamil Nadu. In response to these riots, and on the basis of the report of the Official Languages Commission, the 1963 Official Languages Act was passed (and amended in 1967), continuing the use of English indefinitely. Thus the current official position of English is almost equal to that of Hindi.

In spite of the official position, the Hindi-belt continued to protest against English in what was the Angrezi Hatao ('Banish English') movement during the 1960s.

Several commissions were established in the second half of the twentieth century to look into educational matters. Most of these had ambivalent stances regarding English. Ideologically, English was not favoured but it was seen as necessary. In 1968, the National Policy on Education recommended the three-language formula at secondary school level. In brief, the languages to be learnt were the native language, Hindi and English. If the native language was Hindi, another modern Indian language was to be learnt, preferably one from the south. However, in many states the three-language formula was observed more in the breach. Tamil Nadu resisted Hindi, the north resisted English. Officially, the three-language formula still stands, for school education. Each state determines what actually happens independently. Some states experimented with the removal of or delay in the introduction of English. West Bengal did so in the 1980s as did Karnataka in 2006 but both states brought English back when they saw the disadvantages to their pupils on the national scene, not to mention the international one.

5.2 Indian English pidgins

It is clear that the story of English in India is the story of language debates and the process of institutionalisation in the education system. While there is a certain element of stability to the variety as described in this book, in a language contact situation such as the one that pertains in India, there are other linguistic consequences that must be considered. One of them is the development of pidgins.

Kachru (1994) cites three types of South Asian English pidgins – Babu English, Butler English and Boxwallah English. The first two varieties are better known in India and they are described below.

Babu English (or Baboo English) is the variety of English used by the 'Babu' – a babu was a clerk in the service of the East India Company. Originally used in Bengal, its meaning later included any Indian who wrote imperfect English. This style of Indian English was much parodied. F. Anstey's (Guthrie) works on Baboojee are an example. Appearing first in *Punch* as a series of articles, these pieces were later collected into novels. A few lines from *Baboo Jabberjee* are given below:

> I am this week to narrate an unprecedented stroke of bad luck occurring to the present writer. The incipience of the affair was the addressing of a humble petition to the indulgent ear of Hon'ble *Punch*, calling attention to the great copiousness of my literary output, and the ardent longing I experienced to behold the colour of money on my account. On which, by returning post, my parched soul was reinvigorated by the refreshing draught of a *draft* (if I may be permitted the rather facetious *jeu de mots*) payable to my order. (Anstey 1895: 50)

Being a parody, the work is written mostly in grammatically correct English, and makes use of inappropriate words, idioms and collocations, mixed metaphors, etc. to make its point about Indian English. However, Babu English really refers to examples such as the following letter in which a babu seeks pardon for the behaviour of one of his subordinates:

> Respected Sir,
>
> Kindly excuse to this poor man the once more for his this fault. He is not sort of man to be check [cheeky] to your honour, but being a very fool he not understands the English language. Therefore he spoke you in such way as to look as impertinent.
> Now he is very sorry for the fault which is done by accident, and humbly says no more he will do so again.
> For sake of his families be merciful to him. He has lately been blessed by having a child, do not turn his joy's into misery and sadness.
>
> Yours obedient,
> 15/5/90   W.M. Puttuck
> (J, c 1890: 4–5)

This kind of writing spread to others as well, including those who were not directly clerks. For more examples, see Samples 9, 30 and 37 in Chapter 7.

Butler English has been described in detail by Hosali (1997, 2000). It was the variety of English spoken mostly by the servants of the Madras Presidency. The language is much simplified and the vocabulary items get their own special meanings. Very often, Indian words are used in this kind of speech. The following is an example of Butler English:

> One master call for come India eh England. I say not coming. That master very liking me. I not come. That is like for India—that hot and cold. That England for very cold. I doesn't like it. (cited in Hosali 2000: 241)

An interesting feature of Butler English is that even the British masters simplified their speech in order to be understood by their servants.

Pidgin-like situations exist even in modern India. In small towns that are also great tourist attractions, communication takes place in broken or pidgin English. Temple towns like Madurai, for example, will have a rickshaw-puller saying, 'Very long, saar. Two kilometre. Only ten rupees, saar' to anyone who cannot speak Tamil, the local language.

In the following conversation, A and B are speakers of different Indian languages. A is a proficient user of English whereas B knows a smattering of English. The conversation happened on the phone.

154.

A: I was wondering – where is Rudy?

B: I try, he not picks up, sir.

Further conversation between the two goes like this:

155.

B: When you will come, sir?

A: What do you mean when you will come? I told you no; I can't stand until November.

B: So . . .

A: November- December . . . lot of pain is there. I am taking daily treatment from Doctor.

B: Acchha. Not well-a sir? Kerala treatment . . .

['I see You are not well, is it? What about Kerala treatment?']

A: Kerala treatment . . . yes?

B: Puuraa hai?

['It is complete?']

A: nahi nahi . . .

['No, no . . .']

I am taking this English treatment – physiotherapy . . . they are giving electric current and all that.

Since they do not have a common language, they use a combination of English and Hindi to communicate. Notice that the proficient speaker of English changes his sentence structure to match the structures of the other speaker. 'English treatment' refers to allopathy and related medical systems that come from the West.

5.3 Changes in progress

The case of the pidgin-like situations prevalent today demonstrates clearly that, over the centuries, the linguistic features of IE have been more or less the same. Several works from the earliest times show that IE has always been on a cline of proficiency. Varieties of the kind seen now were apparent even earlier. There was variation at the phonological and syntactic levels and at the level of lexis and discourse. A few changes are apparent from earlier times; some have been discussed in the preceding chapters. A few more features are discussed here.

5.3.1 Spelling

A certain degree of consistency in spelling was seen as desirable by the East India Company. Works that 'interpreted' the Orient to the British were written, such as the one by Stocqueler (1920), which is a compilation of terms (many of which are names of places) whose meanings are provided. Some effort is made to be consistent in spelling. As for pronunciation and the manner in which English spelling attempts to represent it, it has been said that:

> [i]n the orthography of the words, pains have been taken to convey Oriental sounds without resorting to accents or arbitrary pronunciations. The reader is only required to bear in mind, that the letter 'A' *wherever it may occur* is to be sounded as in the interjection 'AH!' (Stocqueler 1920: iv)

British spelling of Indian words attempted to be consistent. Long vowels were represented by writing two letters – *Hindoo, Baboo* etc. This was particularly true of /u:/ which was written as *oo*. As stated above, long /a:/ was not written using two letters. In many words, *aw* was used to represent the same /a:/. Short /a/ was often represented by the letter *u*. This dual representation does lead to some confusion. The sound /k/ was usually written using *c*. Some examples are given below:

> ADAWLUT, justice, equity; a court of justice in India.
> (Stocqueler 1920: 1)

> CARNATIC, CENTRAL or MIDDLE. This Indian province is bounded on the north by the Ceded Districts and the river Pennar...
> (Stocqueler 1920: 51)

GUNGA, The honour of having given birth to this goddess, the personification of the sacred stream of the Ganges, has been claimed for their deities, both by the Saivas and Vaishnavas.

(Stocqueler 1920: 93)

Some examples of sound to spelling correspondence are as follows:

156.

Sound	Letters
/a/	u
/aː/	a, aw
/i/	i, y
/iː/	i, ee
/u/	u
/uː/	oo
/e/	e
/eː/	e
/ai/	ai
/o/	o
/oː/	o
/au/	au, ow
/k/	c, k
/kh/	k, kh
/ʋ/	v, w

After the British left, unofficial attempts have been made to standardise spelling by Indians. Indian languages are more phonetic than English in writing. IE also attempts to be phonetic with regard to words over which it has control. Today, the tendency is to represent /k/ with the letter *k* uniformly. /a/ is represented by *a*. *u* is almost never used in modern Indian spelling for the sound /u/ and *aw* is also completely absent for long /aː/. So what was *Cauvery* is now *Kaveri*. Some residual spellings left by the British do exist such as the use of *ee* for /iː/ as in

Mukherjee. Also, some place names such as Cuddapah and Punjab are the result of earlier spelling. (The former name is now being written as Kadapa.) As a result of these residual elements, *Punjab* is articulated by some people outside the country as /pʊndʒaːb/ rather than the Indian /pəndʒaːb/.

With regard to the spelling of English words in IE, in general, it is British. Thus the overall preference is for *colour, sympathise, fulfilment* and so on. But, with greater American influence it is not unusual to see *sympathize, fulfillment* and other similar words. This influence is particularly seen on the more common *center, labor* and *program*.

5.3.2 Other linguistic aspects

On the whole, there is a tendency to speak without too much concern for standards. This is only to be expected because there is a greater demand for English today in more contexts than there was earlier. People who serve in shopping malls or in ordinary shops – that is, those who are not very well educated – are often in jobs that require English. Consequently, standards are affected.

Pronunciation has evidently been a problem since the early times. Soob Row says in his report:

> As to the pronunciation of the English language it is out of the question that a native can ever be expected to speak it with any degree of fluency. It is therefore, to be supposed that it would be quite sufficient for a native if he could write the language well and grammatically, for it must be admitted that no man can pronounce a foreign language to the fullest degree of fluency and perfection. (Soob Row 1873: 10)

It would certainly not be inaccurate to claim that this state of affairs continues to persist even today but, since pronunciation is considered to be important, schools still teach it. Now, there is a move to change to American pronunciation as the norm, at least in a couple of schools as Nath (2007) notes. With some expatriate Indian families returning to India, it is not uncommon to hear the American accent in the most unexpected places, especially among the younger generation who have been schooled in America.

From the point of view of lexis, the most important change that is occurring is in the use of the words *million* and *billion* replacing the Indian *lakh* and *crore*. Note also the American expression below:

157.

A: How are you?

B: I am good.

Code-mixing within sentences is quite common, especially among younger people. Hinglish which mixes Hindi and English has gained prominence in use. Radio Mirchi is an example of this kind of use. It is no longer unusual to use Hinglish in writing articles as noted by Suman (2007).

In today's India, nobody would deny the importance of both the languages that the Constitution assigned a significant role to – Hindi and English. Hindi has become an extremely useful language to know while communicating with the common person in the country. Whether in Hindi-speaking regions or elsewhere, Hindi is useful on the streets. Hindi has managed to gain this position not because of educational efforts but almost completely due to Bollywood.

The following prophetic words of Macaulay say it all for modern India:

> In India, English is the language spoken by the ruling class. It is spoken by the higher class of natives at the seats of Government. It is likely to become the language of commerce throughout the seas of the East . . .
>
> Whether we look at the intrinsic value of our literature, or at the particular situation of this country, we shall see the strongest reason to think that, of all foreign tongues, the English tongue is that which would be the most useful to our native subjects. (Macaulay 1835)

In keeping with the pluralistic tradition of India, attempts are being made to provide all facilities in as many languages as possible. While earlier, all bills were available only in English, now, utility companies, for instance, offer to send bills in the language chosen by the customer. Still, English, in contrast to Hindi or other Indian languages, has the potential to provide material gain, in the form of lucrative jobs in India and overseas. It is a much sought-after language for these reasons and English teaching institutes, many of dubious status and quality, are seen in every part of the country. Consequently, there is not much to be heard by way of anti-English rhetoric in the country today, even from the Hindi belt. India's software boom has been made possible because of knowledge of English and those who oppose English are aware that a whole new world of riches that has opened up for the country in the last two decades or so will just collapse if the language is lost.

Notes

1. Probably the first Englishmen who came to India were the emissaries of King Alfred in the year 883, as the following extract from the Anglo-Saxon Chronicle shows:

   A.D. 883: This year went the army up the Scheldt to Conde, and there sat a year. And Pope Marinus sent King Alfred the 'lignum Domini'. The same year led Sighelm and Athelstan to Rome the alms which King Alfred ordered thither, and also in India to St. Thomas and to St. Bartholomew. Then they sat against the army at London; and there, with the favour of God, they were very successful after the performance of their vows. (The Avalon Project 2007)

2. The treatise is called *Observations on the State of Society among the Asiatic Subjects of Great Britain, particularly with respect to Morals; and the Means of improving it.*

6 Survey of Previous Work and Annotated Bibliography

Most works on IE do not deal with just one aspect at a time – they touch upon as many features as possible. A greater amount of work has been done on phonology, especially the regional varieties of Indian English, than on other aspects. Lexis is commented on in many works. Syntax is the least studied of all the linguistic features. It is only in the more recent works that we find a deeper analysis of the syntactic structures of IE. The trend among these later works seems to be to try to identify preferences based on the corpora available. The earlier works of the 1960s and 1970s have been more concerned with the idea of establishing whether such a phenomenon as IE exists at all. The most vociferous champion of IE as a legitimate variety of English has been B. B. Kachru.

This chapter lists some of the more important works on English in India and Indian English. It does not purport to be a complete list. There are several articles in different places which deal with similar topics as those covered below. The chapter is divided into parts that somewhat match the chapterisation of the book. The works presented in this chapter are divided according to subject matter. However, perfect categorisation is not possible because, as stated above, many works deal with several aspects at the same time.

6.1 Comprehensive/general works and bibliographies

Aggarwal (1982), *English in South Asia: A Bibliographical Survey of Resources*
The book contains a fairly long introduction by Braj Kachru. The entries, numbering 1181, are divided across chapters into bibliographies, works on history, linguistic structure, literature, pedagogy etc. The book aims to be as comprehensive as possible on English in South Asia. Many of the works are on India. Several works listed are unpublished and there are many dissertations.

Baumgardner (1996), *South Asian English*
The work is divided into four parts, dealing with aspects of identity, structure, function and teaching of South Asian English. Some of the chapters deal with India; the ones on structure, pragmatics and cultural meaning are likely to be of interest.

Bolton and Kachru (2007a), *Asian Englishes: Vol. I, South Asian English, 1837–1938*
This is a collection of thirteen chapters written between 1837 and 1938, of which two are by Indians. The chapters deal with politics, policy and linguistic features. This volume, along with the others in this series is useful in making available works that may otherwise be inaccessible.

Dasgupta (1993), *The Otherness of English: India's Auntie Tongue Syndrome*
This work is highly theoretical in its analysis of English in India. The attempt is to locate the language in a sociolinguistic and cultural hierarchy. The author argues that English has a position similar to the earlier status of Sanskrit. Other Indian languages do not belong in the high domain of English. Consequently, it is above the ordinary and remains the 'other' to which one merely listens because of its high, enthroned status.

Dustoor (1968), *The World of Words*
This is one of the few works that deals, at some length, with Indian English. The work brings together some earlier writings by the author, with the two on Indian English being written specifically for this volume. The work begins with a discussion of words in English in general. One chapter is devoted to Shakespeare's use of language, in particular his vocabulary, and another to a discussion of American English.

A major portion of the work is devoted to Indian English, introducing the background and commenting on the different kinds of words that one encounters in Indian English. The work identifies Indianisms in the use of phrases and set expressions, and some other aspects of morphosyntax. It also discusses aspects of Indian English pronunciation. One chapter is devoted to the divergences of pronunciation from RP. As in all works of slightly earlier times, a somewhat prescriptive approach is seen in the work, especially in the description of pronunciation. The work critiques Indian English for its high style and lack of colloquialism, but is itself written in a pedantic style.

Glauser et al. (1993), *A New Bibliography of Writings on Varieties of English, 1984–1992/3*
This work contains a section with a list of references to works on different aspects of Indian English.

Goffin (1934), 'Some notes on Indian English'
This work provides some of the characteristic features of educated IE. It covers lexis, some grammatical features, and style. It touches very briefly upon the pronunciation of Indians. It is reprinted in Bolton and Kachru (2007a).

Kachru (1983), *The Indianization of English: The English Language in India*
This is a fairly comprehensive book. Along with the historical and sociolinguistic contexts, the overall focus of this book is on the processes that make English Indian and it touches upon lexis and mophosynatax. As the author himself says, the work is a compilation of essays written over a period of time and is therefore uneven in style, presentation and methodology. Some chapters are more for linguists and others more for the uninitiated.

Kachru (1989), *The Alchemy of English*
In this collection of ten chapters, the author draws extensively upon examples of non-native varieties of English; many examples come from India. The work is primarily an attempt to provide a theoretical basis for the analysis of non-native Englishes. The main arguments in the work are that second-language varieties have their own legitimacy and linguistic features. The author devotes considerable space to discussing attitudes towards these varieties and what the pedagogical models of English should be.

Kachru (1994), 'English in South Asia'
This is a very useful chapter which gives an overview of all aspects—history, education, politics and linguistic features—in a comprehensive manner. Although it is supposed to be on English in South Asia, the chapter focuses primarily on India. Most of the linguistic features described also tend to be from India, particularly North India. It also gives details of some varieties of South Asian Englishes which are determined on the basis of function, region and proficiency. The chapter also deals with the impact of English on South Asian languages at the level of lexis and grammar, and the literatures.

Krishnaswamy and Burde (1998), *The Politics of Indians' English*
This work claims to be 'a data-based socio-linguistic perspective on the role of English in India' (v). It criticises the previous work done on Indian English and English in India. The main argument is that a distinction needs to be made between Indian English and English in India and that researchers do not often do so. The authors prefer to use 'Indians' English' because they do not believe that a distinct variety of Indian English exists. Their argument comes from an examination of written samples of English. The work contains several samples from different periods in Indian history and argues that the style of Indians' English has changed over the centuries. It further argues that the domains in which English is used in India have expanded over the centuries but its use is still restricted to only some aspects of Indian life. They use the term 'modulect', in preference to 'dialect' or 'variety', to describe Indians' English.

Parasher (1991), *Indian English: Functions and Form*
This socio-linguistic analysis of English in Indian bilingualism begins by giving a theoretical background. It discusses the notion of Indian English, and by means of extensive field study, establishes the extent to which English is used in various domains. Social factors and language attitudes are also examined. A few aspects of the linguistic features of IE are touched upon.

Parasher (1999b), 'Remarks on Indian English'
In this work, the author considers the question of what Indian English is. He traces the history of the expression 'Indian English', and treats it as a product of language contact. He provides the typical linguistic features of what he calls 'educated Indian English'. Yet, he considers it to be lower than native varieties of English, since it is a second language variety.

Ramaiah (1988), *Indian English: A Bibliographical Guide to Resources*
This bibliography is among the first of its kind for Indian English. It contains 1015 entries of work done up to 1987. The entries are placed in ten sections: bibliographies, generalia, linguistic aspects, lexicons, lexis and vocabulary, borrowings, phonology, grammar, errors and stylistics.

Sridhar (1989), *English in Indian Bilingualism*
This collection of ten chapters discusses English in the Indian context from a sociolinguistic point of view. The author determines the extent of bilingualism and variation and the use of code-mixing in different parts of the country.

One chapter provides a history of English education in India. Some chapters are theoretical in nature, while others are data based. One of them is an empirical study of strategies of requesting in IE. Another considers the language used in V. S. Naipaul's early novels.

6.2 Phonetics and phonology

Bansal (1976), *The Intelligibility of Indian English*
This work examines the intelligibility of twenty-four Indian speakers' English, using different types of test material, to users of English from different backgrounds. The features of IE are described, especially the segmental features. The work is significant in that it is among the first detailed works on IE phonetics and, in turn, inspired a number of dissertations in India on intelligibility studies.

Chaudhary (1989), *Some Aspects of the Phonology of Indian English*
An attempt is made in this work to give a comprehensive account of IE stress and some other related phonological processes. It is argued that the stress patterns of IE are based on the language family of the speakers' language. The author provides a set of syllabification rules for Maithili English which is extended to other varieties of IE and a syllable strength hierarchy is proposed. In addition, some other rules are seen to be necessary (such as spelling rules and lexical rules) that make some syllables heavy. The different language groups interpret words differently for syllabification, particularly in the manner in which medial clusters are distributed.

Stress rules apply to the strings generated by the rules of syllabification and stress is sensitive to quantity. Feet are constructed on words following a metrical system of phonology that was then current. In general, stress is placed on the first foot in Dravidian language Englishes and on the second foot in Indo-Aryan language Englishes, which accounts for the respective pronunciations of *'asparagus* and *aspa'ragus*.

CIEFL (1972), *The Sound System of Indian English*
This is a short monograph of just sixteen pages based on research carried out by Colin Masica. It is a quick introduction to the overall phonemic and phonetic features of generalised Indian English which, according to the author, seem to have become the de facto norm. It identifies the consonants and the vowels used in IE and some of the variations that occur based on region. The monograph has five sections of which the last is prescriptive in nature. The work sets up a prescriptive standard that is close to the generalised IE that is described in the text.

Gargesh (2004), 'Indian English: Phonology'
This is also a brief introduction to educated IE pronunciation and it describes its distinctive consonants and vowels using lexical sets. Some of the phonological processes in IE are described and a short analysis of the prosodic features is provided.

Thundy (1976), 'The origins of Indian English'
This work begins by pointing out the similarities between American and Indian English. But, it maintains that American English did not influence IE, rather the speakers who came from the various parts of UK did. This hypothesis is backed up by pointing out the similarities between IE phonology and the different speech forms of Ireland, Scotland, the north-west Midlands and Cockney.

6.3 Morphosyntax

Agnihotri et al. (1988), *Tense in Indian English: A Sociolinguistic Perspective*
This large-scale project on the use of tense by 356 undergraduate sixteen- to eighteen-year-olds studying in different types of colleges in Delhi shows that the overall command of the use of tenses with appropriate function is rather low. Those who come from better colleges are better in their overall performance. The work establishes an implicational order of difficulty in the acquisition of tenses and has a distinct pedagogical orientation.

Bhatt (2004), 'Indian English: Syntax'
The work makes a distinction between standard Indian English and vernacular Indian English and discusses some syntactic features of the latter. It argues that these features are systematic and should not be perceived as deviant. Further, the argument here is that the grammar of the culture must be taken into account in discussing these aspects. The syntactic features discussed are: direct and indirect questions, in relation to the process of subject-auxiliary inversion, tag questions, topicalisation, the focus particle *only*, pro-drop, and null expletive subjects.

Parasher (1983), 'Indian English: Certain grammatical, lexical and stylistic features'
Although some features of lexis are touched upon, the work focuses primarily on syntax and style. A fairly large sample of letters and reports from two institutions was collected and given to speakers of different varieties of English – British, American and Indian – for acceptability

judgements. The work concludes that, at the syntactic level, the differences between IE and other native varieties are minimal and that the major differences are at the level of lexis and style.

Verma (1978), 'Syntactic irregularities in Indian English'
This work lists some of the common non-standard pan-Indian syntactic usages of English. The examples are of inter-clause tense concord, conditional sentences, indirect questions, tag questions, tense and aspect, *wh-*questions, *want + that* clauses, responses to questions, use of the progressive with stative verbs, word order, relative clauses, collocation and some typical IE lexical items. The argument, despite the title, is that there is a structured system in IE and IE is non-native because of its similarity to other non-native varieties of English.

Whitworth (1907), *Indian English: An Examination of the Errors of Idiom made by Indians in Writing English*
This work is meant to be an aid to Indians in correcting their errors of grammar and usage so that their English may be even better than it is. It focuses on the usual aspects of Indian English expression such as articles, adverbs, adjectives, nouns, verbs and sentence structure. It is very likely that later works used this as a model for their description of Indian English. Most of the comments made are still relevant in modern Indian English and, today, this work may be seen as providing examples of what we mostly call non-standard Indian English. Some items have passed into standard IE. The work has been reprinted in Bolton and Kachru (2007c).

6.4 Discourse, lexis, lexicons and glossaries

Gumperz et al. (1982), 'Thematic structure and progression in discourse'
This is a detailed analysis of IE data in which discourse features are compared with English as spoken by westerners. The differences are pointed out and the underlying reasons for the discourse features of IE are discussed. Many aspects of syntax are covered in the chapter and it is shown how a specific syntactic structure derives from the discourse in which it is uttered. The features of IE are compared to features of Indian languages particularly Hindi, in order to show why IE discourse works the way it does.

Hawkins (1984), *Common Indian Words in English*
This is a short volume containing about 2000 words and is meant for those interested in India or those who live there. Some words of English origin but with an Indian meaning are also included.

Kachru (1975), 'Lexical innovations in South Asian English'
This work deals with the South Asian element in English. Although the title refers to South Asia, most of the words come from India, more particularly from North India. Since Hindi, Hindustani and Urdu have contributed more to the lexis of (Indian) English, this may perhaps be expected. After an introduction to lexis in South Asia and its impact on English, the work, which is 'data oriented', provides a large number of examples of words that are South Asian in origin. They are categorised into single items and hybrid items. The latter are dealt with in some detail in terms of collocations, lexical sets, ordered series of words and reduplication. Examples of hybrid items with the South Asian element in the modifier position and in the head position are provided.

Muthiah (1991), *Words in Indian English: A Reader's Guide*
This short volume of about 2000 words attempts to make Indian English accessible to foreigners and to students. It is a glossary that includes Indian words and Indian English words that are used commonly in India and gives their meanings.

Nihalani et al. (2005), *Indian and British English: A Handbook of Usage and Pronunciation*
This is an interesting work and probably the only one of its kind to compare British and Indian English. It is divided into two parts – the first one dealing with usage and the second dealing with pronunciation. The two parts have separate introductions. Part I contains about 1000 words bringing out the differences in usage and meaning of words between British and Indian English. Part II contains about 2000 words which illustrate the different pronunciations in the two varieties. Although the work sets out to be descriptive, the introduction to Part II is by the authors' own admission, prescriptive. The Indian variety of English described (for pronunciation) is called IRP—Indian Recommended Pronunciation.

Sengupta (1996), 'A supplement of Indian English'
This is a modern attempt at providing a dictionary for Indian English. As stated in the preface to the supplement, different types of words have been included in the list: words from Indian languages expressing uniquely Indian ideas; words from Indian languages that are used in IE even though native English words exist for the same concepts; English words used differently in India; and usages and idioms peculiar to the country. Although a useful reference tool, this compilation has the same problem that other such attempts would have – all the words cannot be considered to be pan-Indian.

Subba Rao (1954), *Indian Words in English*
This work is short yet thorough in its analysis of the Indian words that have gone into English over the centuries. It is probably the only work of its kind that analyses so comprehensively Indian words in English and the reasons for the assimilation. The work provides a list of all the major words in each century. The phonetic changes, the grammatical classes and word formation associated with such assimilated items and the semantic changes that have taken place in the transfer are detailed. One chapter is devoted to the use of Indian words by English men of letters. The story of these words, according to the author, often reveals 'the strange story of Indo-British cultural relations through the centuries, from the viewpoint of the English' (100). The description is followed by a list of the words that have been assimilated into English. This work has recently been reprinted in Bolton and Kachru (2007c).

Whitworth (1976), *An Anglo-Indian Dictionary*
This work, first produced in 1885, is similar to the work done by Yule and Burnell (see below), but has not secured the same recognition as that work did, probably because it merely gives the meanings of words whereas the other volume gives early sources and quotations and is much more detailed. For those just looking up meanings of words, this work would have been of use. The origin of a word is also provided.

Yule and Burnell (1986), *Hobson-Jobson*
This substantial volume of 1886 is often cited as an authoritative source for Anglo-Indian words. The term Anglo-Indian itself deserves some discussion – it was the expression used for the British who lived in India. Much later, the term began to mean people who were of mixed blood.

The glossary is different from many previous glossaries which were directly functional. This is a general purpose, historical dictionary of the words that either found their way into the English language from India or were words that were used in India. Though rather dated (since many of the words that are said to be specific to the location are no longer used), it is still considered to be a primary resource on Indian words.

The title, quite deliberately chosen for its interest value, is the version of the Muslim cry during Moharram 'Ya Hasan! Ya Hosein!' as heard by English ears. It is also an indicator of the extent to which phonological changes can and do take place when words are carried over from one language to another. The dictionary is available in a searchable, digital form at Yule (2006).

6.5 History, education and politics

Bolton and Kachru (2007d), *Asian Englishes: vol.4, Debating English in India, 1968–1976*
The volume is a compilation of two works on the post-independence debates regarding English in India. The first chapter is a reprint of Shah (1968). Shah's work brings together speeches made and statements issued inside and outside parliament, by Members of Parliament, ministers, newspaper editors and other opinion makers. The immediate reason for the debate was the Education Minister's proposal in July 1967 that the regional language should be the medium of instruction in higher education.

The second chapter by Chatterjee (1976) summarises the different opinions with regard to English education in India, especially the Anglicist-Orientalist debate.

Garg (2001), *Policy Documents on Indian Education*
The volume brings together some of the major and minor original documents that were relevant in the Indian context, which are especially focused on Indian education, beginning with Warren Hastings' 'Minute' of 17 April 1781. Most of them have a relevance to English starting from about 1781 up to 1945. The work also contains such documents as Macaulay's 'Minute', Prinsep's 'Note', Wood's Education Despatch of 1854, Hunter's Indian Education Commission of 1882, documents relating to Lord Curzon's educational policy of 1904 and Indian Educational Policy 1913. It is a useful resource containing the important texts in their original form. While the documents are useful, the narrative leaves a lot to be desired.

Law (1915), *Promotion of Learning in India by Early European Settlers*
This work deals with the history of education in India up to about 1800. It provides details about the various schools that were set up and their students, schooling systems and finances. The work also discusses the libraries and the printing activities that the Europeans undertook. While some references are made to Bombay, Goa and Calcutta, the main focus of the book is the Madras Presidency. It gives a detailed account of the Bell system of education.

Ram (1983), *Trading in Language: The Story of English in India*
This work is a history of English in India and contains a detailed analysis of some key players and documents in the making of this history, beginning with Charles Grant and Macaulay's 'Minute'. The final document examined in detail is the Report of the Radhakrishnan Commission. The

work laments the fact that English has been made such an important language in India and concludes by elaborating in detail the cases of USSR and Britain which managed to keep an indigenous language and minimise the importance of foreign languages. The work is excellent in critiquing the documents and in analysing the background of important personalities.

Mahmood (1981), *A History of English Education in India (1781–1893)*

This voluminous work is a very detailed account of the official position and efforts of the East India Company and the British Government regarding education from 1781 to 1893. It includes several documents in their entirety or in large portions and is, perhaps, the most authentic and comprehensive work of the period. It tries to adopt a neutral tone in the representation of facts. The most valuable contribution of this book is that it provides painstakingly compiled data, dealing with the demographics of English education and providing projections on the absorption and spread of the language.

Sinha (1978), *English in India*

This is a comprehensive study of English education in India tracing the origins to the Portuguese systems before the advent of the English. It details the relevant political events and the course of English education and touches briefly upon the years after independence.

Sonntag (2000), 'Ideology and policy in the politics of the English language in North India'

This is a well-researched chapter in which the author describes in detail the ebb and flow of the language discourse in North India that commenced nearly a hundred years ago. The positions taken by different political groupings with regard to the three main contenders for leading language – English, Hindi and Hindustani – have been detailed along with the accompanying political events. The author concludes that, while an ideologically directed analysis may help in understanding the current status of the discourse, it will not necessarily help in predicting the contours of future events.

Trevelyan (1838), *On the Education of the People of India*

This book gives an account of the events and discussions that took place immediately before and after Macaulay's 'Minute'. The work has a clear Anglicist orientation but is valuable for the details it provides. It deals with not just general education but all aspects, including, for example, medicine.

6.6 Samples and corpora

D'souza (2001), 'Contextualizing range and depth in Indian English'
This is a data-orientated work drawing from a wide range of popular writings particularly to demonstrate that IE exists in different forms and at different levels. It seeks to adduce data that counter the 'otherness of English' approach taken by some scholars, such as Dasgupta (1993) and Krishnaswamy and Burde (1998), by letting the data speak for themselves. The data cover code-mixing, lexis, sentence structures and other miscellaneous aspects.

J. (c. 1890), *Baboo English*
This is a collection of several specimens of writings by Indians in a style that came to be termed Baboo English during British times. The items were collected over twenty-five years. The compiler says that the samples are drawn from the writings of educated Indians, who have passed an English examination at the university. The samples are gathered from letters, applications, advertisements, telegrams, notes and so on. This work is reprinted in Bolton and Kachru (2007b).

Mehrotra (1998), *Indian English: Texts and Interpretation*
After a brief introduction to English in India and Indian English, the work contains a large collection of samples drawn from various genres and domains. The samples are divided across chapters on literary texts, lectures, newspaper articles and miscellaneous material. There are samples also from different varieties of Indian English, which are non-standard and are examples of broken English and hybridised English etc. The samples are followed by comments on them. The work is useful for those who want different kinds of examples from Indian English.

Nelson (2007), *International Corpus of English* – India
This corpus of IE is an interim release and is a section of the larger International Corpus of English. The India section consists of five hundred texts, both written and spoken.

Shastri et al. (1986), *The Kolhapur Corpus*
Modelled on the Lancaster Oslo/Bergen Corpus and Brown Corpus for British and American English, the Kolhapur Corpus is computer based and consists of samples from Indian English of the year 1978. There is a total of 500 texts from different categories such as: the press, including reportage, editorials and reviews; religion; skills, trades and hobbies;

popular lore; belles lettres; miscellaneous items (which include government documents, reports and other material); learned and scientific writings; general fiction; mystery and detective fiction; science fiction; adventure and western fiction; romances and love stories; and humour.

Wright (1891), *Baboo English as 'Tis Writ*
This work also focuses on Baboo English but, this time, the items are taken from Indian journalistic writing. It provides an introduction to the Indian press. The samples are from editorial announcements, notices in the papers, reports, petitions and letters to the editor. The items are used to comment on the nature of Indian journalism in general and the style of writing as well. This work is now reprinted in Bolton and Kachru (2007b).

7 Sample Texts

The samples in this chapter are divided according to domains of use. They are drawn from a wide range of topics and represent samples of written and spoken forms across the centuries. Samples of the different varieties of IE – standard Indian English and non-standard – are interspersed below. It is evident here that different degrees of proficiency existed earlier, much as they do in modern times. Brief comments are given where relevant. The wide range that exists in the grammar, lexis and style of IE is demonstrated to some extent in this chapter.

7.1 Literature

Literature is written in standard English and is devoid of non-standard constructions, as (1) below shows. Where non-standard or 'Indian' constructions are used, it is done with a deliberate purpose.

1. 1794: *The Travels of Dean Mahomet*

Dear Sir,

Having remained some time in Dacca, we proceeded on our voyage to Calcutta, and, in about two days reached the river Sunderbun, which is extremely narrow, and winds into many branches, that feast the delighted eye with a variety of new scenery: the land on each side is low, and covered with great trees, close to the water's edge: the water was smooth and transparent when we passed through, and appeared like an extended mirror reflecting the tall trees that grew upon each border. Creation seemed to be at rest, and no noise disturbed the silence which reigned around; save, now and then, the roaring of wild beasts in the adjacent woods: the scene was truly great, and raised into unaffected grandeur, without the assistance of art.

The most remarkable trees that grow on each margin of the river, are the sandal, aumuooze, and ceesoe. The woods are infested with ferocious animals of different kinds, which frequently destroy the unwary traveller; and the tygers in particular are daring enough to approach the river side, and dart on the very passengers in the boats going up and down, of whom they make an instant prey. Along the banks are many villages, at about ten or twelve miles distance from each other, where we sometimes laid in a fresh supply of provisions. There is no display of art in the construction of the collages, which are only composed of broad green flags fastened together, and supported by frames of bamboes. (Mahomet 1794: 141–3)

The sample is from the first English book published by an Indian author. It is in the form of letters, giving an autobiographical account of the life and experiences of an Indian who was an employee of the East India Company. The author had travelled considerably, and finally married and settled in Britain. This work is written in standard English and has no features that might mark it as Indian.

2. 1938: *Kanthapura*

Our Rangamma is no village kid. It is not for nothing she got papers from the city, *Tai-nadu, Vishwakarnataka, Deshabhandu,* and *Jayabharatha,* and she knows so many, many things, too, of the plants that weep, of the monkeys that were the men we have become, of the worms, thin-as-dust worms that get into your blood and give you dysentery and plague and cholera. She told us, too, about the stars that are so far that some have poured their light into the blue space long before you were born, long before you were born or your father was born or your grandfather was born; and just as a day of Brahma is a million million years of ours, the day of the stars is a million million times our day, and each star has a sun and each sun has a moon, and each moon has an earth, and some there are that have two moons, and some three, and out there between the folds of the milky way, she told us, out there, there is just a chink, and you put your eyes to a great tube and see another world with sun and moon and stars, all bright and floating in the diamond dust of God. And that gave us such a shiver, I tell you, that we would not sit alone in the kitchen that night or the night after. (Rao 1974: 40–3)

Raja Rao is among the first three big names of Indian English fiction, along with R. K. Narayan and Mulk Raj Anand. In this piece from his novel *Kanthapura,* he deliberately Indianises English in the sentence structure, which consists of long utterances and repetitions, to bring out the Indian flavour.

3. 1975: *Ramana Maharshi*

The great event which formed a turning point in the life of the Maharshi and in modern man's quest for identity took place in the middle of July 1896, perhaps on Thursday, July 16th (*shukla paksha shashti*), about six weeks before he left Madurai for good. One day he was sitting alone on the first floor of his uncle's house (11, Chokkappa Naicken Street, near the temple). He was in good health and yet felt a sudden and unaccountable fear of death. This turned his mind inward and he pursued an enquiry somewhat like this: 'Now I am dying, what does this death mean? What is it that is dying? This body dies'. He dramatized the act of death, extended his limbs and made them rigid, held his breath and kept his mouth closed. He continued the silent enquiry: 'Well then, the body is dead. It will be carried stiff to the burning ground and there burnt and reduced to ashes. But am I dead? Is the body I? The body is silent and inert, but I feel the full force of my personality and even hear the voice, the *sphurana*, of the "I" within. Hence I am awareness transcending the body. I am the spirit immortal'. All this enquiry was not an intellectual exercise but a living experience of the pure 'I am' awareness which he went through viscerally without words.

The vivid dramatization of death which transformed a schoolboy into a sage may be viewed under the terms of mythology, metaphysics and morals. Less like the creaturely Elephant King who was saved from imminent death by a motherlike Vishnu, the sustainer of dharma, and became a supreme bhakta, and more like Sankara who was freed from another crocodile and turned into a master-thinker by Father Siva, the god of transcendent awareness, young Venkataraman during his clear calm acceptance of the body's end discovered his inmost being as pure awareness and thus overcame once for all the fear of death. (Swaminathan 1975: 8–9)

A professor of English, K. Swaminathan was also an author and translator. In this biography of the spiritual teacher, Ramana Maharshi, he describes the most significant moment in the Maharshi's life. Writing on spirituality invariably necessitates the use of Indian words. This example draws from Hindu philosophy and mythology, but does not contain too many culture-specific words. See (20) below for an example from music.

4. 1982: 'The Patriot'

> I am standing for peace and non-violence
> Why world is fighting fighting,

Why all people of world
Are not following Mahatma Gandhi,
I am simply not understanding...
All men are brothers, no?
In India also
Gujaraties, Maharashtrians, Hindiwallahs
All brothers –...
You are going?
But you will visit again...
Always I am enjoying your company.

(Ezekiel 1992: 268–9)

Considered to be among those who defined Indian English poetry, Nissim Ezekiel deliberately parodies Indian English in a set of poems called *Very Indian Poems in Indian English*, of which this is one example. Non-standard features of IE morphosyntax are used in this piece.

5. 1989: *The Great Indian Novel*

'Then tell me, Krishna, what should I do? How can I seek to win her?'

'You *are* one for medieval chivalric conventions, aren't you? Subhadra has always said she'd choose her own husband, but from what I've seen of her I doubt very much she'd able to judge what was for her own good. My advice would be quite simply to give her no choice. Be Valentino, not Valentine. Kidnap her. Take her away on a white charger!'

'You mean—elope?'

'You make it sound so prosaic, Arjun,' Krishna sighed in eye-twinkling resignation. 'But yes, I suppose I do mean elope. Except that if eloping involves the consent of both parties, abduction might be a lot more effective.'

Startled, Ganapathi? Not quite the way for a good Indian elder brother to behave, eh? If you thought that, I suppose you'd be right, but this was just one more instance of Krishna's innocently instinctual amorality. He lived by rules which originated in an ancient and ineffable source, a source that transcended tradition. Unlike the rest of us, even unlike Arjun, Krishna found his basic truth within himself. No conventional code could confine the joyous surging force of vitality, of essential life, that he embodied.

And so the plans were laid; Arjun borrowed a white Ambassador car to serve as his charger, and lay in wait after dark along the route Subhadra used on her way back from her evening classical-music lessons. (Tharoor 1989: 331–2)

Shashi Tharoor's *The Great Indian Novel* is a take-off on the Indian epic the *Mahabharata*. The novel recreates modern Indian history in the framework of the epic. It is written in a conversational style using modern idiom. Other than the use of names and allusions that are Indian, the language does not carry any features of non-standard IE.

6. 1999: *Wings of Fire: An Autobiography*

In 1979, a six-member team was preparing the flight version of a complex second stage control system for static test and evaluation. The team was in countdown mode at T-15 minutes (15 minutes before the test). One of the twelve valves did not respond during checkout. Anxiety drove the members of the team to the test site to look into the problem. Suddenly the oxidizer tank, filled with red fuming nitric acid (RFNA), burst, causing severe acid burns to the team members. It was a very traumatic experience to see the suffering of the injured. Kurup and I rushed to the Trivandrum Medical College Hospital and begged to have our colleagues admitted, as six beds were not available in the hospital at that point of time.

Sivaramakrishnan Nair was one among the six persons injured. The acid had burned his body at a number of places. By the time we got a bed in the hospital, he was in severe pain. I kept vigil at his bedside. Around 3 o'clock in the morning, Sivaramakrishnan regained consciousness. His first words expressed regret over the mishap and assured me that he would make up the slippage in schedules caused by the accident. His sincerity and optimism, even in the midst of such severe pain, impressed me deeply.

Men like Sivaramakrishnan are a breed apart. They are the strivers, always reaching higher than the last time. And with their social and family life welded to their dream, they find the rewards of their drive overwhelming – the inherent joy of being in flow. This event greatly enhanced my confidence in my team; a team that would stand like a rock in success and failure. (Kalam 1999: 89–91)

This piece, by a former President of India, Abdul Kalam who was known as the People's President, is simple in language and style and is representative of writing more commonly seen today.

7.2 Official documents and other letters

Many official documents, including annual reports, were in the form of letters. Most of the ones below are in standard IE, except for an occasional Indian structure.

7. 1788: Letter by a Judge, Ali Ibrahim Khan, to Lord Cornwallis reporting a battle

17th October 1788

I have already sent you two letters giving an account of the situation at Shahjahanabad. I now write for your information what further intelligence I could gather from the papers of news. On 9th October 1788, corresponding to 8 Muharram 1203, Rana Khan and other Maratha sardars, forming confederacy with Mirza Ismail Beg Khan, delivered a combined attack on the fort and forced an entrance into it. A free fight ensued between them and the defenders of the fort, in which both the sword and the gun were used. At last the Marathas succeeded in seizing Manyar Singh kumedar (Commandant), a dependant of Ghulam Qadir Khan, who led the defence. Both sides suffered heavy casualties. Rana Khan then released the Emperor Shah Alam from the room in which he was confined by Ghulam Qadir Khan, who had barricaded its door before he fled. Rana Khan treated the Emperor with great respect and honour. The Marathas are now holding the fort. Ghulam Qadir is encamped with his army on the other side of the Jamna. He is short of provision and a Maratha force has surrounded him. (Khan 1936: 323–4)

This is an example of how Indian words were used in British India even when corresponding with British officials. In some cases, translations were used as in the case of *Commandant* but not for other words like *sardar*. It is intriguing that the date is also described in the Muslim way by referring to Muharram, especially considering that it was written to a British official.

8. 1828: Letter from His Highness, the Rajah of Tanjore, to A. D. Campbell

My Dear Sir,

It is with sincere pleasure that I acknowledge the receipt of your friendly Letter of the 27th June last, which has been handed to me on the 6th instant, by Bagvunt Row, the manager of the Board of Revenue, of whom you speak so favourably in the same. I received him with pleasure, and showed him the mark of my kindness. He appears a good-natured, clever, and honest man – much attached to your friendship. His conversation and manner, which were very pleasing, made me to believe that what was written, by you, about his merit, is but too little. He will come and tell you, with what sense of gratification I always remember you, and your kindness to me, during your short stay at Tanjore – it is such that I cannot forget through life. But the only thing which gives me great anxiety, and sorrow is, that you are not even in your former situation at Madras, though not appointed, as I should wish, in this country. Wherever or in whatever station you may be, I have no doubt you will bear a particular interest in the welfare and comfort of this your distant friend.

That you may enjoy long life, health, comfort and happiness is, and will always be, the particular wish and prayer of,

My Dear Sir,
Very affectionately yours,
SERFOJEE RAJAH

Tanjore, 7th August, 1828

(Rajah 1828: 34)

This piece has Indian features such as 'made me to believe' and 'the same'. These are used quite a bit in IE today as well. The last line is culturally very Indian in that it elaborately wishes the other well.

9. 1890: Complainant against a fellow workman

To

Mr. J – Esq.

Sir,

I most respectfully beg to lay before your honour the following few complaint which by your mercy I can get satisfaction.

That the Basan Blacksmith working on one and threw the iron on my foots, by that reason it is much painful and unfit for movement; by this reason I am his enemy because he is nothing knowing the work of line, whenever he is doing any mistake then I prohibited him, for this reason he always telling I will see you. Now he ruin me and done on my foot injury, for which I am incapable, and you will kindly transfer to other place, and ever remain.

W. D.

20/3/90

(W. D. c. 1890: 3)

This is an example of Babu English, which was a variety of English used by Indian staff, particularly during the British period.

10. 1924: Report

To
The President and Members of the Managing Committee of the Watson Museum of Antiquities, RAJKOT.

WATSON MUSEUM OF ANTIQUITIES
Rajkot, 18th September, 1924.

Gentlemen,
I have the honour to submit the following annual report on the working of the Museum for the year 1923–24 . . .

BRITISH EMPIRE EXHIBITION.

Dewan Bahadur T. Vijayaraghavacharya, Exhibition Commissioner for India, visited the Museum and made a very careful selection of articles from the Museum to be sent to the British Empire Exhibition, London. The articles were selected by him but the Committee's approval was obtained before the same were sent to the British Empire Exhibition. These articles were sent to London in three boxes specially prepared for the purpose. The expenses on this head all told have upto now amounted to Rs.490–8–6. All expenses on account of this have to be borne by the States and so a bill will be sent to them when at the close of the Exhibition expenses on account of the return of the articles are sent to me by the Exhibition Commissioner for India. The items spent up to now have been debited to a special account opened in the Museum books for the British Empire Exhibition . . .

I would bring to the notice of the Committee the admirable efforts which the Curator is putting forth in the research work. The part-time clerk Chhotalal Kanji inspite of his small remuneration is also doing his part of the ordinary work of the Museum in a most satisfactory way.

I have the honour to be,
Gentlemen,
Your most obedient servant,
Vithaldas G. Trivedi
Honorary Secretary
(Trivedi 1924: 1 and 8)

This piece is written in standard English using complex structures quite comfortably. Notice the use of 'the same' here as well.

7.3 Newspaper articles and reports

The following items are drawn from different newspapers published across the country.

11. 1875

Just as we were going to press we received for insertion copy of a petition of the inhabitants of Dinagepore to His Honor the Lieutenant Governor, praying for the retention of Mr. Robinson the late Relief Commissioner of Dinagepore in that district, whom it is stated the Government proposes to appoint Commissioner of Chota Nagpore. The petitioners speak very highly of the services of Mr. Robinson, and would consider it a great loss if he were withdrawn from the district. Whether their prayer be granted or not the testimony borne by them to Mr. Robinson's qualifications and character is very flattering, and we dare say is fully deserved. ('Editor's note' 1875: 32)

This piece from *The Hindoo Patriot* is a fine example of the felicitous use of English quite early in time. Yet the article *a* is not used before 'copy'.

12. 1941

MADRAS, MAY 24.
Madras experienced the hottest day so far of the present season to-day, a maximum temperature of 107.4 degrees being recorded a little after 1–15 p.m. This figure exceeds by over a degree the highest temperature recorded for May last year (106 degrees on May 12). ('Hot weather in the city'1941: 3)

It is interesting that temperatures are given in Fahrenheit in this news item. In India today the norm is to use Centigrade.

13. 1950

All Delhi is agog today, giving finishing touches to the arrangements connected with the celebrations of the Republic Day, the highlights of which are the swearing-in ceremony at the Durbar Hall in Government House of Dr. Rajendra Prasad as the first President of the Republic, and the Presidential drive along a five-mile route to the Irwin Stadium, where the new head of the State will unfurl the National Flag.

Peasants, politicians, Princes and diplomats from far and wide are already pouring into the city to witness this epoch-making event, and the whole city wears a festive air with arches and bunting, flowers and flags, while, at night, it will be transformed into a fairyland by bushes and trees floodlit by multi-coloured electric bulbs.

The day will dawn with 'prabhat pheries' going round different localities, while the President-elect himself will begin his day with prayers and a visit to Rajghat to pay homage to the Father of the Nation. ('Birth of Indian republic' 1950: 1)

This piece from *The Times of India* on the occasion of the Republic Day celebrations in 1950 is written in standard IE. The lone Hindi expression is placed in quotation marks to indicate that it is a different language. Such marks are not used in writing today. Words from Indian languages are used freely as some of the samples in this chapter show. 'Father of the Nation' refers to M. K. Gandhi.

14. 1953

Dharwar, Dec 31:
Mr. S. Nijalingappa, President of the Karnatak Pradesh Congress Committee, has voiced a strong protest against the allotment of only one day for Karnatak in the tour programme of the Ramamurthy Committee appointed by the Centre to tour the famine areas of South India. He says that no useful purpose will be served by such lightening tour and adds that it was Karnatak which took the initiative in October last and urged the appointment of a committee to formulate schemes to deal with the problems of the dry belt in the South, frequently liable to famine, on a permanent basis.

So, it was surprising that Karnatak had itself been now relegated into background in the tour programme of the committee. 'It is such acts of scant attention and indifference to our problems that makes us sick and yearn for a separate state soon,' Mr. Nijalingappa remarked. He has appealed to the Committee to spare more time for Karnatak. ('Famine team's tour' 1953: 9)

Here, 'lightening' is used for 'lightning' and an article is missing before 'lightening tour'. The compound *dry belt* refers to areas that are devoid of water.

15. 1953

Ahmedabad, February 1: Mr. V.N. Chandavarkar, former Vice-Chancellor of Bombay University, 'confessed' today that he found it too difficult to write out his first Convocation address due to 'lack of scholarship and incompetence to deliver speeches.' It was like preparing for an examination, he said. ('Convocation speech was difficult job' 1953: 9)

Non-standard IE uses *too* in the sense of 'very'. *This is too good* means that it is extremely good. This feature is percolating into standard IE as well.

16. 1965

Thiruchirappalli May 5 (PTI)
Workers digging a well in the little known village of Devimangalam in Udayarpalayam Taluk in Tiruchi district, found a pot containing gold coins.
The treasure trove – 106 gold coins – has been deposited in the taluk office at Jayagondam. ('Gold coins found' 1965: 4)

This piece contains names that would be difficult for those not familiar with them. *Taluk* is a smaller unit than a district, used for administrative purposes.

17. 1972

CHANDIGARH: A joke current in Chandigarh about Haryana Cabinet these days is: 'ek mantri, baqi sub santri' (one Minister, all the rest are sentries). This is to say that the only Minister is MR. BANSI LAL, while other members of his nodding cabinet are mere sentries around him.
These remarks were, for the first time, heard during MR. KAIRON'S 8-year-regime when Chief Minister Kairon ruled over composite Punjab with an iron hand and carried his cabinet of yes-men with him. Things in Haryana are, more or less, analogous to those days. ('Mantris & Sentries' 1972: 2)

This is an interesting example of the way in which Hindi jokes are used in English newspapers in India. But it is not assumed here that everybody will understand the joke and it is explained immediately. The expression *nodding cabinet* refers to *yes-men*.

18. 2006

Saturday night was rocking because just about everybody decided to have a party that day. Ramesh Ramaya had a boat party, which left most of his good friends in a shock. Nothing scandalous happened, it's just that they didn't get an invite. This is really odd because these five guys are generally invited to every party Ramesh hosts. When his friends asked him he said, 'I thought you guys were going to Brij Sahani's place.' Brij had a get together at her new place in Jubilee Hills . . .

Even though so much was happening over the weekend the die-hard party animals were not tired. Some of the older lot rushed off to Ahala after they finished with the private dos. The ones at Jay Galla's places stayed put though till the wee hours.

Although the guests were having a jolly good time, the poor hosts didn't have it so easy. Hyderabadis always accept all the invites that come their way and then hop from one place to another at their own whim and fancy leaving the poor hosts flustered. ('Saturdays are real fun' 2006: 44)

This item is extremely informal in nature and is representative of the language used in writing about social events and gossip.

19. 2007

There are only two instances of anything remotely clever in *Red*, and one is the fact that Neel (Aftab Shivdasani) has a hole in his heart and he spends his days glancing at his wristwatch, at the time he has left. (Get it? His life revolves around . . . tickers.) The other moment comes when Neel gets well, and he looks up information about a woman (Anahita, played by Celina Jaitley) who's recently lost her husband. He goes to the web site of the *Hindustan Times*, and he sees a picture of her with the caption, 'The *Greiving* Widow.' (Get it? It's a cunning commentary on the abysmal standards of English in the media today.) Oh okay – in either case, my interpretations aren't probably the intentions of director Vikram Bhatt, but this is what you do while watching a bad movie. You try to make it more interesting for yourself, directorial vision be damned. I needn't have strained my brain to this extent had only the rest of *Red* worked on the level that Jaitley does. She gives one of those deliciously atrocious performances that sets mind-boggling standards for the rest of the film to live down to, and had *Red* only taken up the dare, we'd have had ourselves that rarest of things: a genuine guilty pleasure. But Bhatt is too chicken, and all we're left with is a flat-out bore. (Rangan 2007: 7)

This review of a film is written in a conversational, informal style which is quite common for this type of writing.

20. 2007

Komanduru Venkatakrishna is one of the best violin accompanists in Andhra, and following the footsteps of his father, Seshadri, he too chose to become a vocalist cum violinist. He is currently working as a lecturer in violin at Venkateswara Music College, Tirupati. Venkatakrishna was recently in town to give a vocal concert for Hyderabad Music Circle and Thygaraya Gana Sabha, who arranged the program jointly last week.

Krishna began the show with *Vasantha raga varnam* and went on to *Swaminatha Paripalayamam* of Deekshitar in *Nata* an invocation. He added wonderful swarakalpana to it that also exercised his sharpened his voice. He then rendered *Devininnu Brova* of Shyama Sastry in a rare *raga Chintamani*.

The *kirtana* came off well with a melodic lilt. He took up *Arabhi* for brief sketch and sang *Chala Kallaladukonna* of Thyagaraja, rendering the lines in different *sangaties* to make literary impact. This was also marked by a good *swarakalpana*. He then rendered *Pranaamamyaham* in *Ranjani*, a rarely rendered composition in *misrajati Triputa tala*. *Srisankaraguruvaram* in *Nagaswaravali* served as a relief number before the major melody *Thodi*, for the popular composition of Thyagaraja *Kaddanu Vaariki*. (Srihari 2007: 3)

This review of a vocal concert is obviously incomprehensible to all but those who have knowledge of the terminology of Indian classical (Karnatic) music. None of the Indian words has a satisfactory English equivalent.

21. 2007

Not many know that during the Mughal times, wine was elevated to an art form. Early European travellers to the courts of Mughul emperors Akbar, Jehangir and Shahjehan in the sixteenth and seventeenth centuries reported to having tasted the 'best wines in the world' from the royal vineyards. Red wines were made from the arkesham grape and white wine from arkawati and bhokry grapes.

Under British influence in the nineteenth century, vineyards were established in Kashmir and at Baramati in Maharashtra and a number of Indian wines were exhibited and favourably received by visitors to the Great Calcutta Exhibition of 1884.

However, Indian vineyards were totally destroyed by phylloxera in the 1890s. It took nearly half a century to replant them. Today, lineal descendants of some of these historic wines are produced by Chateau Indage, India's largest producer of wine, as well as by Grover Vineyard, Sula and Shaw Wallace.

India has now 123,000 acres of vineyards, but only one percent of them is used for wine. However, that does not mean the wine market in the country isn't maturing. Today the overall sales are around 400,000 cases a year. Table wines account for 85 per cent of the market and expensive varieties of vintage wines account for the remaining 15 per cent. (Khosla 2007: 59–60)

This piece is written in standard IE.

22. 2007

Fourth phase of the National Badminton camp, aimed at preparing medal winners at the 2010 Commonwealth Games at New Delhi, is on at the Saroornagar Indoor Stadium and some of the players who were on the 11-player Indian team that toured Germany, England and Switzerland are expected to report in a couple of days.

The camp will conclude on April 8 and according to National coach P. Gopi Chand, different types of coaching is being imparted to different sections of players. ('Shuttle camp in full swing' 2007: 42)

An article is missing at the beginning of the item. *Indoor* could be a typographical error but need not necessarily be that. Spacing between words tends to be somewhat erratic in IE. Subject-verb concord is missing in the last sentence.

7.4 Letters to the editor

The letters are written in standard IE but they contain an occasional Indian word or non-standard construction.

23. 1965: 'Ban on skirt'

Sir—The report that the sari is to replace the customary blouse and skirt for top-standard girls of the Huzurpaga High School, Poona, is disturbing. Physical education of girls cannot be subjected to greater neglect than it is at present.

Saris worn by school girls will further prevent what little exercise they are permitted. That little girls must wear dresses below the knee reveals a shocking attitude of prudism.

Is there something vulgar in the lovely bare legs of a child? Is it not commonsense to restrict clothing of children to the minimum in a hot climate, to say nothing of giving the freedom to run, jump and skip? Are we trying to raise healthy women or dolls?

When the late Professor Haldane described the sari as the symbol of slavery of Indian women, he certainly hit the nail on the head. The sari is very beautiful, but for all practical purposes it is useless, and must take its share of blame for the poor standards of physical fitness of the fair sex.

Mrs. Sathe, the school superintendent, says it is surprising that Western dress (sic) is replacing the sari in India. What is surprising about this fact? Cumbersome national costume almost all over the world has been replaced by simplicity of dress for obvious reasons except in very backward countries. May I suggest that the Huzurpaga High School carries its back-dated ideas to their ultimate conclusion and veils its students, so that the antics of roadside Romeos be curtailed forever? If Mrs. Sathe is a progressive educationist, heaven preserve us from the backward ones.

WINFRED BOSE
AHMEDABAD

(Bose 1965)

'Top-standard' refers to the higher classes in school, and the expression 'roadside Romeos' is used in India to refer to boys who tease girls on the streets. 'Prudism' is used in place of prudery.

24. 1987: 'Mercy missions'

Sir,–The article by P. M. Bakshi (June 16) was very educative. He has elucidated the exceptions to the principles of territorial autonomy, international law having come to recognise the paramount importance of alleviating human suffering, thereby granting impunity, so to say, to actions taken on humanitarian grounds.

If the obligation to protect the sanctity of human life, its very survival, is universally accepted, why do mercy missions not exist to prevent the starvation deaths in our own country? Does charity not begin at home any more?

Sheela Dandekar
Bombay

(Dandekar 1987)

This letter is written in standard IE and does not carry any non-standard features.

25. 1987: 'Last call'

Sir, This is the last call to nationalised banks to improve their customer service.
Otherwise, Indians will have no alternative but to open accounts with Swiss banks!

Bombay
Homi A Kharas

(Kharas 1987)

The comment on Swiss banks is something Indians would relate to immediately. Most ill-gotten wealth especially of politicians is said to be stowed away in Swiss banks.

26. 1994: 'Bridging tongues'

I read some articles on translations and the problem of communication across various Indian languages in the October-November issue of *IRB*.

We worry about a national language in India. What would be much more useful is a national or common script. This is because various groups of languages have some common and many similar words. A Marathi reader would understand most of a Gujarati and much of a Bengali book written in the devnagari script. A Telugu reader would understand a good part of a Tamil book written in the Telugu script. Obviously, a Malayali would not understand Urdu poetry simply because it is written in the Malayalam script. But a common script will increase the stock of words in each language and bring the languages closer together over a period of time. The politicians have not thought of this solution simply because they are illiterate. Literate and educated Indians could perhaps take it up.

What could be better for airing this kind of an untested hypothesis than *IRB*.

Aparna Tulpule
Bombay 400 068
(Tulpule 1994)

This letter is an example of how concerned Indians tend to be with regard to language, which is a very emotive issue.

27. 2006: 'Ways to make autos safe for passengers'

This has reference to your article, 'Women harassed on Necklace road' in the *Hyderabad Chronicle* dated December 11. I appreciate the advice given by the police department to note down the auto number, keep a cellphone handy and file a complaint with the police. Here, I request the police and RTA officials to ensure that all the autos and taxis have their registration numbers written or painted in front of the passenger seats along with the police control room telephone numbers. This should be made mandatory as it is in Delhi, Chennai and Bangalore.

Last week an auto driver misbehaved with me and when I wanted to note his number he pushed off and there was no number at the back of the auto. There are times when a passenger who's in a hurry gets into the auto without clearly noting the number. I hope the concerned officials will take notice and impose fines on autos and taxis that do not have proper licence plates or that don't display registration numbers and police control room numbers.

V. Rajagopal, *Secunderabad*
(Rajagopal 2006)

Here is an issue that many Indians would relate to given the unreliable nature of public transport in the country. *Autorickshaws*, abbreviated to 'autos', are three-wheeler vehicles available for hire to the public.

7.5 Advertisements

Advertisements use language in many interesting and novel ways. A number of them use abbreviations freely.

28. 1875

TO LET

No. 5 & 7 Kristodas Pal's Lane Baranusy Ghose's Street fit for residence for native gentlemen with family. Apply to Printer.

('To let' 1875)

The word 'native' here means an Indian and obviously implies that it is not suitable for a European.

29. 1890

NITYA NANDA BISWAS' JEWELLERY &

PODDARY SHOP.

Rampore Bazar, Boaleb, Raj's halihye.

All sorts of gold, silver and jewelled ornaments are kept ready for sale and also made to orders at cheaper rates than others. Confident of the superior quality of the articles and the comparatively moderate prices at which they are sold, I invite comparison and challenge competition. For particulars see illustrated catalogue, price 6 pice including postage.

('Nitya Nanda Biswas' jewellery' 1890)

The expression 'made to orders' is non-standard, in an otherwise confident piece of writing.

30. c. 1890

PERPETUAL MOUSE TRAP

Always it requires no failing, and catches continually so long any remains.
('Perpetual mouse trap' c. 1890: 132)

This is an example of Babu English.

31. 1912

MINERVA THEATRE
6, Beadon Street
Wednesday, the 1st May at 8.30 p.m
Mr. D. L. Roy's Grand National Drama
RANA PROTAP

Rana Protap-Surendra Nath Ghose
(my humble self)

Sakto Singh – Mr. N. Banerjee (amateur)
Akbor – Babu Preo Nath Ghose
Prithwiraj – Babu Monmotho Nath Pal
Meherunissa – Sm. Nori Sundari
Joshi bai – Sm. Tara Sundari

To be followed by
G. C. Ghose's magnificent Opera
PARISANA.

Parisana – Sm. Nori Sundari
Full of Sublime Songs and Graceful Dances

C. C. Bose   S. N. Ghose
Bus. Mgr.   Manager.
(Bose and Ghose 1912)

This early advertisement for a play uses expressions such as 'my humble self'. The characters and the cast are listed here. One of them is identified as an amateur artiste.

32. 1953

CASH YOUR
COMMONSENSE

MUST BE WON
IN

COMMONSENSE
CROSSWORD
No. C-3

For full particulars see
The Illustrated
Weekly of India

of
January 25th, February 1st & 8th
('Cash your commonsense' 1953)

The use of 'cash' as a verb is interesting in this advertisement.

33. 1961

ABDULLA
are the best
Virginia
cigarettes

EVERY ABDULLA NO. 7 IS A FULL SIZE CIGARETTE
('Abdulla' 1961)

This simple advertisement has no non-standard features.

34. 1965

MATRIMONIAL

Wanted well-placed young men in Civil or Defence Services 26–28 years from respectable Andhra Non-Brahmin families preferably Kapus for two beautiful and accomplished girls (1) 22 years B.Sc. England-Returned (2) 19 years Higher Secondary Delhi — Father Senior Class I Officer Central Govt. Please write to . . .

('Matrimonial' 1965)

Newspapers and magazines in India contain several matrimonial advertisements. Most of them give details about the background and community as the example here does. 'England-returned' is a non-standard compound.

35. 1972

> THE MOST STOLEN
> MAGAZINE OF THE CENTURY
> Stolen in Post, Railways,
> Offices and Homes.
> MOTHER INDIA
> Edited by
> BABURAO PATEL
> Rs.3/- per copy
> SEPTEMBER ISSUE
> AT ALL BOOK STALLS.
> ('The most stolen magazine of the century' 1972)

This advertisement catches readers' attention by being amusing.

36. 2007

> Teachers & Professors
>
> *offered*
>
> Eng Trainer, f, smart, expd/ fresher, having good comucn skills, sal. Nego . . .
> ('Teachers & Professors' 2007)

This advertisement uses a number of abbreviations, the full forms of which are understood from the context.

7.6 Miscellaneous

37. c. 1890: 'Remarks copied from the visitor's book at an up-country museum'

In Friday I was come to see your Honours Museum at A.M and very much pleased to see all objects, and specially I was very much wonderful to see the largest snake amongst all the things; there was a short of time for me to leave, and I was obliged *to stop writing*. ('Remarks' c. 1890: 69)

This is another example of Babu English.

38. 1995: Recipe, 'Rote'

Castor sugar 250 gm	Ghee (frozen) 125 gm
Sooji 500 gm	Milk ¼ ltr
Saffron a pinch	Rose essence ½ tsp
Chopped almonds 2 tbsp	Chopped cashewnuts 2 tbsp
Raisins 2 tbsp	Poppy seeds 2 tbsp

METHOD

Beat the sugar and ghee till frothy. Add sooji and milk alternately to avoid lumps. Heat 1 tbsp milk and soak the saffron in it, then add it to the sooji-milk mixture. Add nuts together with the rose essence. Grease a large thali and set the mixture in the centre and pat it at the top to level it, leaving the edges free for it to spread while baking.

Sprinkle poppy seeds on top and bake in a moderate oven for 20/25 minutes. Cool and cut into desired shapes. (Mehta 1995: 15)

In this recipe the author makes use of Hindi and English words randomly. Not all of these words would be comprehensible across all language groups. While 'thali' which means 'plate' may be understood, 'sooji' which is 'semolina' is not likely to be.

39. 2006: Student Writing

There are two major tests in language testing. One is subjective testing. It involves tester's subjectivity in evaluation. This kind of test may not have reliability, because, marks may not be the same when the two testers evaluate the paper. A testee may not get same mark or same performance, when the testee attempts second time. The testee is provided instructions to perform the test. It is very easy to construct it and difficult to evaluate for the tester.

Second major type of testing is objective testing. It involves scoring. It is very easy to perform the test for the testee and it is very difficulty for a tester to construct the objective type test. The tester feels easy to evaluate this kind of testing. The tester must be careful in preparing distractors for this type of tests. This kind of test is useful to conduct a test on large group in a limited time. (From a post-graduate student answer script 2006)

This non-standard writing is from the script of a non-proficient user of English. Non-standardness is apparent in the manner in which articles and verb complements are used.

7.7 Lectures

The extracts from lectures below are all in standard IE and are from the speeches of proficient users of English.

The first piece (40) is one of the series of lectures Swami Vivekananda gave at the World's Parliament of Religions, Chicago. This lecture was delivered on 15 September 1893.

40. 1893: 'Why we disagree'

I will tell you a little story. You have heard the eloquent speaker who has just finished say, 'Let us cease from abusing each other,' and he was very sorry that there should be always so much variance.

But I think I should tell you a story which would illustrate the cause of this variance. A frog lived in a well. It had lived there for a long time. It was born there and brought up there, and yet was a little, small frog. Of course the evolutionists were not there then to tell us whether the frog lost its eyes or not, but, for our story's sake, we must take it for granted that it had its eyes, and that it every day cleansed the water of all the worms and bacilli that lived in it with an energy that would do credit to our modern bacteriologists. In this way it went on and became a little sleek and fat. Well, one day another frog that lived in the sea came and fell into the well.

'Where are you from?'

'I am from the sea.'

'The sea! How big is that? Is it as big as my well?' and he took a leap from one side of the well to the other.

'My friend,' said the frog of the sea, 'how do you compare the sea with your little well?'

Then the frog took another leap and asked, 'Is your sea so big?'

'What nonsense you speak, to compare the sea with your well!'

'Well, then,' said the frog of the well, 'nothing can be bigger than my well; there can be nothing bigger than this; this fellow is a liar, so turn him out.'

That has been the difficulty all the while.

I am a Hindu. I am sitting in my own little well and thinking that the whole world is my little well. The Christian sits in his well and thinks the whole world is his well. The Mohammedan sits in his little well and thinks that is the whole world. I have to thank you of America for the great attempt you are making to break down the barriers of this little world of ours, and hope that, in the future, the Lord will help you to accomplish your purpose. (Vivekananda 1985: 2–3)

41. 1960: 'From early times upto the 19th century'

I deem it a great privilege that I should have been asked to deliver the third of the memorial lectures which have been instituted in the name of that great son of India, Dadabhai Naoroji. To the present generation perhaps, the name of Dadabhai Naoroji may not mean as much as it did to those of us of an older generation. His contributions in many fields of public activity are too numerous to mention; but, during his whole life-time, the passion for progress in his own country was such that whatever position he occupied the interests of his country were always foremost. Thrice President of the Indian National Congress, a Member of the British Parliament, one whose advice was eagerly sought after by his countrymen at all times, Dadabhai Naoroji lived to the ripe old age of 91 and has left to his grateful countrymen a record and a career which might well be an example and an inspiration for the younger generation.

His interest in matters pertaining to education and more particularly to the education of girls and women of India was profound...

When I was asked therefore to deliver these lectures, I confess I felt some hesitation, not because of any lack of admiration for this great Indian statesman but due to the diffidence whether I could perform the task with any degree of competence as befits the memorial founded to commemorate such a great personality. Discretion might have been the better part of valour but, having accepted your invitation, I place myself in your hands and crave your indulgence for these few lectures that I have been privileged to deliver. (Mudaliar 1960: 1–3)

42. 1996: 'The empowerment of women'

The new world into which you are going is very complex. It is hungry for peace having witnessed the greatest bloodshed in this 20th century than in all history. The conquest of science over man and elements has revolutionized life. We talk today of genetic engineering, prevention of diseases, cure for the most incurable. We have used the same progressive science to eliminate life in terms of highly sophisticated weapons. In the very recent past we watched the Gulf war sitting in our drawing rooms. It is equally easy to take the help of an ultrasonic device to determine the gender of a foetus and discard it if it is not of one's choice, i.e. a girl.

Science has conquered distances and shrunk the world to a tiny place. You can tele-conference sitting in your drawing room with another sitting across the globe. You can travel round the world faster than the earth revolves around the Sun. Yet, those that know no letters nor have the facility of any infrastructure have to spend long hours fetching fuel, water, fodder and wake up with the Sun to go back to sleep when the Sun sets. (Gopalan 1996: 17)

43. 2007: *Beyond Liberal Humanism and Technological Transhumanism*

I am standing in front of you this afternoon to share with you my anguish at the state of the world we live in today and to describe to you briefly how I had to struggle to find my moorings once again in Sri Aurobindo and the Mother. This world has always been a Kurukshetra, a field of battle, on which the forces of good and evil keep contending ceaselessly, but thanks to the inspired words of Sri Aurobindo and the Mother, most of the time I have been able to detect a silver lining behind the dark clouds and some basis for inner hope and certitude. For me to believe in the Divine is to be a voluntary optimist, no matter how depressing the world around us.

Recent times have been particularly bleak. The events in the Middle-East are extremely disturbing. Israel's savage assault against the Hizbollah in Lebanon offers one way of combating terrorism and the world seems to understand and even applaud this way. Contrast this with our own softer way, which does not seem to be working any better than the hard way. The recent bomb-blasts in local trains in Mumbai, are another reminder that India is probably not faring very well in its fight against terrorism either because it is too sentimentally 'non-violent' and goody-goody or because its political will as a nation is too splintered for any cohesive and resolute action. One wonders if India has the political will to get its act together and be united even when confronted with the grave threat of terrorism to its very existence. (Nadkarni 2007: 1–2)

7.8 Audio samples

The audio samples accompanying this volume attempt to provide a few examples of the speech of IE. Variation in the speech of IE is demonstrated through these samples. Transcripts of two of the samples are given below. These are very close to SIEP. The other samples represent different varieties that are found in different parts. Readers can access the audio files by clicking on the link at http://lel.ed.ac.uk/dialects/.

The first sample (44) below is that of a seventeen-year-old girl who was educated in Madanapalli and Hyderabad.

44. Ira

You'll probably notice that I'm really short, that's probably the first thing you'll notice, and like ma'am says, I'm usually pretty loud in classes. uh But, I can be really quiet when I want to, most people don't believe that either. Uh [laughs] I . . . According to me, sports are really hazardous to health, so I stay away as far from the sports complex, as far as I can; even cycling is very frustrating. I love reading books, and . . . usually called a book-worm . . . at my old school. That's my favourite pastime. [laughs] Okay, I'm usually dancing around; I love dancing. Uh I seem to have this tendency of banging into things, which led to the name . . . give giving me the name of a walking-talking disaster waiting to happen.

The speech is very close to SIEP described in Chapter 2 and retroflex sounds are heard in words like *dancing* and *tendency*. The word *frustrating* has /ə/ in the first syllable. *Ma'am* refers to the speaker's teacher, who is present, and is an example of younger speakers not using the names of older people or teachers.

The next audio sample is that of a speaker who is twenty-two years old and is located in Delhi.

45. Deepti

So we now came to uh this part of Delhi, which is north Delhi, from the village which is rural Delhi. I certainly had this uh accent as well as the language of uh that part of Delhi, rural Delhi, which is Haryanvi of sorts; it is a uh dialect, and I . . . I did face problems in the sense, that you know I . . . I went to a school where people spoke . . . uh mm you know, sort of, fashionable Hindi I can say, and I was talking in a, uh, bad Hindi, . . . bad uh I mean you know, it was not even Hindi. So people used to be like you know, she is talking in some alien language. Even my neighbours they took some time to accept that okay she is somebody; and uh they would ask my parents every time . . . they were . . . a word they did not understand . . . th . . . a simple thing like a ball . . . we would call it a *gindo*, which is a *geend* in Hindi . . . so *geend* is sort of uh made a *gindo* uh converted, the word is *gindo* for *geend* in Haryanvi. So, these were the things that I . . . I faced problems for a year or two I guess, but then, my parents were there, my family . . . most of my family was settled here, and then they made it a point that even when they are talking in the . . . uh inside home, and it's a personal conversation, they, they would not use such colloquial words, they would be using proper Hindi words so that I get accustomed to it. So, uh then they put me in a school which was of a Hindi-medium till fifth standard, so that I am, you know, I have a base. It was a very well thought-out thing my dad did, maybe my mother; so, I went to that school, then I had a base in Hindi first. And I faced problems getting into English. I, for for my sixth standard I had my science in English, so in the first unit test I flunked. Because I just did not know how to express myself in English and I thought that you know, learning is not a way out. Because uh when I was writing exams till fifth standard, I would never learn. I would just know a thing and I would write about it. So uh in sixth standard I wou flunked in my science exam – first unit test. Then I had a tutor, tutor as in there was this girl who used to come to my mother to, uh, study uh she was a student, of my mother; so she sat down to teach me science. Then from there I took it up and till tenth standard I had a nice grasp of English. In 11th and 12th, it was again better, and I had no clue that I would be taking up English ever in my life.

This is also a very neutral accent and close to SIEP in that there are no regional features to reveal the background of the speaker. The degree of retroflexion is greater in this speech. The phonological features of Indian English as described in Chapter 2 are apparent here. It is non-rhotic and linking /r/ is present. Unexpectedly, /ɖɪ/ is used where /ɖə/ would be used in *the language*. The word *learn* is used in the sense of 'memorising' or 'rote-learning' here. The discourse features are the use of *sort of*, *I mean* and *you know*.

Bibliography of Cited Works

'Abdulla', advertisement (1961), *The Times of India*, 27 December.
Aggarwal, Narinder K. (1982), *English in South Asia: A Bibliographical Survey of Resources*, Gurgaon: Indian Documentation Service.
Agnihotri, R. K., A. L. Khanna and A. Mukherjee (1984), 'The use of articles in Indian English: Errors and pedagogical implications', *International Review of Applied Linguistics in Language Teaching* XXXII:2, 115–28.
Agnihotri, R. K., A. L. Khanna and A. Mukherjee (1988), *Tense in Indian English: A Sociolinguistic Perspective*, New Delhi: Bahri Publications Private Limited.
Agnihotri, R. K. and Anju Sahgal (1985), 'Is Indian English retroflexed and r-full?', *Indian Journal of Applied Linguistics* X1:1, 97–108.
Alam Ara, film, directed by Ardeshir Irani, music director B. Irani and F. M. Mistri, India: Imperial Movietone, 1931.
Algeo, John (2006), *British or American English? A Handbook of Word and Grammar Patterns*, Cambridge: Cambridge University Press.
Anstey, F. (n.d.), *Baboo Jabberjee, B. A.*, London: J. M. Dent & Sons Ltd.
Arnold, Alison (2000), 'Film music: Northern area', in Alison Arnold (ed.), pp. 531–41.
Arnold, Alison (ed.) (2000), *The Garland Encyclopedia of World Music: vol. 5, South Asia: The Indian Subcontinent*, New York: Garland Publishing, Inc.
Asiatic Society, The (2007), 'History'. Online: http://www.asiaticsocietycal.com/history/index.htm
Avalon Project, The (1996–2007), 'The Anglo-Saxon Chronicle: Ninth century', *The Avalon Project at Yale Law School: Documents in Law, History and Diplomacy*. Online: http://www.yale.edu/lawweb/avalon/angsax/ang09.htm
Bansal, R. K. [1969] (1976), *The Intelligibility of Indian English*, Monograph No. 4, Hyderabad: Central Institute of English and Foreign Languages.
Bansal, R. K. (1978), 'The phonology of Indian English', in Ramesh Mohan (ed.), pp. 101–13.
Bauer, Laurie (2002), *An Introduction to International Varieties of English*, Edinburgh: Edinburgh University Press.
Baumgardner, Robert J. (ed.) (1996), *South Asian English: Structure, Use, and Users*, Delhi: Oxford University Press.
Bhatia, Tej K. (1987), 'English in advertising: Multiple mixing and media', *World Englishes* 6:1, 33–48.

Bhatt, Rakesh M. (2000), 'Optimal expressions in Indian English', *English Language and Linguistics* 4: 1, 69–95.
Bhatt, Rakesh M. (2004), 'Indian English: Syntax', in Bernd Kortmann, Kate Burridge, Rajend Mesthrie, Edgar W. Schneider and Clive Upton (eds), *The Handbook of Varieties of English: vol. 2, Morphology and Syntax*, Berlin: Mouton de Gruyter, pp. 1016–30.
'Birth of Indian republic to be proclaimed today' (1950), *The Times of India*, 26 January.
Bolton, Kingsley and Braj B. Kachru (2007a), *Asian Englishes: vol. 1, South Asian English, 1837–1938*, London: Routledge.
Bolton, Kingsley and Braj B. Kachru (2007b), *Asian Englishes: vol. 2, 'Baboo English', 1890–1891*, London: Routledge.
Bolton, Kingsley and Braj B. Kachru (2007c), *Asian Englishes: vol. 3, Features of Indian English, 1907–1954*, London: Routledge.
Bolton, Kingsley and Braj B. Kachru (2007d), *Asian Englishes: vol. 4, Debating English in India, 1968–1976*, London: Routledge.
Bose, C. C. and S. N. Ghose (1912), 'Minerva theatre', advertisement, *The Hindoo Patriot*, 1 May.
Bose, Winfred (1965), 'Ban on skirt', letter to the editor, *The Indian Express*, 30 April.
Boss, film, directed by V. N. Aditya, music director Kalyani Malik, India: Kamakshi Studio, 2006.
'Cash your commonsense', advertisement (1953), *The Times of India*, 24 January.
Chatterjee, Kalyan K. (1976), *English Education in India: Issues and Opinions*, Delhi: Macmillan.
Chaudhary, Shreesh C. (1989), *Some Aspects of the Phonology of Indian English*, Ranchi: Jayaswal Press.
Chaudhary, Shreesh C. (1996), 'Speaking to the global village: Towards globally usable accents of English', *CIEFL Bulletin (New Series)* 8:2, 29–58.
Chib, Som Nath (1936), *Language, Universities and Nationalism in India*, London: Oxford University Press.
CIEFL (1972), *The Sound System of Indian English*, Monograph No. 7, Hyderabad: Central Institute of English and Foreign Languages.
'Circulation pattern of English newspapers in India' (2007), *indiastat.com*. Online: http://www.indiastat.com
Constitution of India, The. Online: http://www.constitution.org/cons/india/const.html.
'Convocation speech was difficult job' (1953), *The Times of India*, 2 February.
Criminal, film, directed by Mahesh Bhatt, music director M. M. Kreem, India: Mukesh Bhatt, 1995.
Dandekar, Sheela (1987), 'Mercy missions', letter to the editor, *The Times of India*, 2 July.
Das, Shyamal (2001), *Some Aspects of the Prosodic Phonology of Tripura Bangla and Tripura Bangla English*, unpublished PhD dissertation, Hyderabad: Central Institute of English and Foreign Languages.
Dasgupta, Probal (1993), *The Otherness of English: India's Auntie Tongue Syndrome*, New Delhi: Sage Publications.

Daswani, C. J. (1978), 'Some theoretical implications for investigating Indian English', in Ramesh Mohan (ed.), pp. 115–28.
Davidson, Keith (2007), 'The nature and significance of English as a global language', *English Today* 89, 23: 1, 48–50.
'Distribution of the Mother Tongues (having a minimum of 10,000 speakers in India) included under the 96 Non-Scheduled Languages' (2007), *indiastat.com*. Online: http://www.indiastat.com.
Dixon, R. M. W. (1991), 'Some observations on the grammar of Indian English', in B. Lakshmi Bai and B. Ramakrishna Reddy (eds), *Studies in Dravidian and General Linguistics: A Festschrift for Bh. Krishnamurti*, Hyderabad: Centre of Advanced Study in Linguistics, Osmania University, pp. 437–47.
D'souza, Jean (1988), 'Interactional strategies in South Asian languages: Their implications for teaching English internationally', *World Englishes* 7:2, 159–71.
D'souza, Jean (1992), 'The relationship between code-mixing and the new varieties of English: Issues and implications', *World Englishes* 11:2/3, 217–23.
D'souza, Jean (2001), 'Contextualizing range and depth in Indian English', *World Englishes* 20:2, 145–59.
Dubey, Vinod S. (1994), 'Lexico-morphological dimensions of Indian English', in R. S. Pathak (ed.), *Indianisation of English Language and Literature*, New Delhi: Bahri Publications, pp. 33–49.
Dustoor, P. E. (1968), *The World of Words*, Bombay: Asia Publishing House.
'Editor's note' (1875), *The Hindoo Patriot*, 18 January.
Ek Duuje ke liye, film, directed by K. Balachander, music director Laxmikant and Pyarelal, India: Prasad Productions Private Ltd, 1981.
'Emerging Indians' (2007), *The Week* 5 August, pp. 8–37.
Ezekiel, Nissim [1989] (1992), 'The Patriot', in N. Ezekiel *Collected Poems: 1952–1988*, Delhi: Oxford University Press, pp. 268–9.
'Famine team's tour: KPCC chief's view' (1953), *The Times of India*, 1 January.
Garg, B. R. (2001), *Policy Documents on Indian Education*, Ambala Cantonment: The Associated Publishers.
Gargesh, Ravinder (2004), 'Indian English: Phonology', in Edgar W. Schneider, Kate Burridge, Bernd Kortmann, Rajend Mesthrie and Clive Upton (eds), *The Handbook of Varieties of English: vol. 1, Phonology*, Berlin: Mouton de Gruyter, pp. 993–1002.
Geisler, Christer (2000), 'Ahmad S. Peyawary, *The Core Vocabulary of International English: A Corpus Approach*, Bergen: The Humanities Information Technologies Research Programme. HIT-senterets publikasjonsserie 2/99', *ICAME Journal* 24, 140–2.
Glauser, Beat, Edgar W. Schneider and Manfred Gorlach (1993), *A New Bibliography of Writings on Varieties of English, 1984–1992/3*, Amsterdam: John Benjamins Publishing Company.
Goffin, Raymond C. (1934), 'Some notes on Indian English', *S. P. E. Tract No. 41*, 20–32.
Gokak, V. K. (1964), *English in India: Its Present and Future*, Bombay: Asia Publishing House.
'Gold coins found' (1965), *The Indian Express*, 7 May.

Gopalan, Sarala (1996), 'The empowerment of women', *University News* 35:13, 17–19.
Government of India (2005), 'Profile', *Know India*. Online: http://india.gov.in/knowindia/profile.php.
Greene, Paul D. (2000), 'Film music: Southern area', in Alison Arnold (ed.), pp. 542–6.
Gumperz, John J., Gurinder Aulakh and Hannah Kaltman (1982), 'Thematic structure and progression in discourse', in John J. Gumperz (ed.), *Language and Social Identity*, Cambridge University Press: Cambridge, pp. 22–56.
Haigh, Chris (n.d.), 'Indian violin', *Fiddling around the World*. Online: http://www.fiddlingaround.co.uk/india/index.html
Hawkins, R. E. (1984), *Common Indian Words in English*, Delhi: Oxford University Press.
'Highlights' (2007), *Registrar of Newspapers for India*. Online: https://rni.nic.in/welcome.html
Hosali, Priya (1997), *Nuances of English in India: What the Butler Really Said*, Pune: Centre for Communication Studies, Indus Education Foundation.
Hosali, Priya (1999), 'The English language in India: its origin(s)', in K. V. Tirumalesh (ed.), pp. 1–15.
Hosali, Priya (2000), *Butler English: Form and Function*, Delhi: B. R. Publishing Corporation.
'Hot weather in the city: last year's record broken' (1941), *The Hindu*, 25 May.
J, T. W. (ed.) (c. 1890), *'Baboo English' or Our Mother-tongue as our Aryan Brethren Understand it. Amusing Specimens of Composition and Style, or, English as Written by some of Her Majesty's Indian Subjects*, Calcutta: H. P. Kent and Co.
Jhankaar Beats, film, directed by Sujoy Ghosh, music director Vishal and Shekhar, India: Pritish Nandy Communications Ltd, 2003.
Julie, film, directed by K. S. Sethumadhavan, music director Rajesh Roshan, India: B. Nagi Reddy and Chakrapani, 1975.
Kachru, B. B. (1965), 'The *Indianness* of Indian English', *Word* 21, 391–410.
Kachru, B. B. (1975), 'Lexical innovations in South Asian English', *International Journal of the Sociology of Language* 4, 55–74.
Kachru, B. B. (1976), 'Models of English for the Third World: White man's linguistic burden or language pragmatics?', *TESOL Quarterly* 10:2, 221–39.
Kachru, B. B. (1982), 'Models for non-native Englishes', in B. B. Kachru (ed.), *The Other Tongue: English across Cultures*, Urbana: University of Illinois Press, pp. 31–57.
Kachru, B. B. (1983), *The Indianization of English: The English Language in India*, Delhi: Oxford University Press.
Kachru, B. B. [1986] (1989), *The Alchemy of English: The Spread, Functions and Models of Non-native Englishes*, Delhi: Oxford University Press.
Kachru, B. B. (1994), 'English in South Asia', in Robert Burchfield (ed.), *The Cambridge History of the English Language: vol. 5, English in Britain and Overseas: Origins and Development*, Cambridge: Cambridge University Press, pp. 497–553.
Kachru, Yamuna (2006), 'Mixers lyricing in Hinglish: Blending and fusion in Indian pop culture', *World Englishes* 25:2, 223–33.

Kalam, A. P. J. Abdul with Arun Tiwari (1999), *Wings of Fire: An Autobiography*, Hyderabad: Universities Press.
Karnad, Girish [1988] (1995), 'India', in Martin Banham (ed.), *The Cambridge Guide to Theatre*, pp. 316–526.
Katikar, P. B. (1984), *The Meanings of Modals in Indian English*, unpublished PhD dissertation, Kolhapur: Shivaji University.
Khan, Ali Ibrahim [1788] (1936), 'Ali Ibrahim Khan, Judge at Benares, to Lord Cornwallis', in Jadunath Sarkar (ed.), *Poona Residency Correspondence: vol. 1*, Bombay: Government Central Press, pp. 323–4.
Khan, Farhat (1989), *Linguistic Variation in Indian English*, unpublished PhD dissertation, University of Reading.
Khan, Farhat (1991), 'Final consonant cluster simplification in a variety of Indian English', in Jenny Cheshire (ed.), *English around the World: Sociolinguistic Perspectives*, Cambridge: Cambridge University Press, pp. 288–98.
Kharas, Homi A. (1987), 'Last call', letter to the editor, *The Times of India*, 23 July.
Khosla, Mukesh (2007), 'Indian wine: What's brewing in the barrel?', *Sattva* 2:3, 58–61.
Kothari, Rita [2003] (2006), *Translating India: The Cultural Politics of English*, New Delhi: Foundation Books Private Ltd.
Krishnamurti, Bh. (1978), 'Spelling pronunciation in Indian English', in Ramesh Mohan (ed.), pp. 129–39.
Krishnaswamy, N. and Archana S. Burde (1998), *The Politics of Indians' English: Linguistic Colonialism and the Expanding English Empire*, Delhi: Oxford University Press.
Kumar, Ashok (1986), 'Certain aspects of the form and function of Hindi-English code-switching', *Journal of Anthropological Linguistics* 28:2, 195–205.
Lagaan, film, directed by Ashutosh Gowariker, music director A. R. Rahman, India: Aamir Khan Productions Ltd, 2001.
Lal, Vinay (2007), 'Indian fusion music', *Manas*. Online: http://www.sscnet.ucla.edu/southasia/Culture/Music/fusion.html
Law, Narendra Nath (1915), *Promotion of Learning in India by Early European Settlers*, London: Longmans Green and Co.
Lukmani, Yasmeen (1992), 'Indian English: The written record', in Claudia Blank, Teresa Kirschner, Donald Gutch and Judith Gilbert (eds), *Language and Civilization: A Concerted Profusion of Essays and Studies in Honour of Otto Hietsch: vol. 2*, Frankfurt-on-Main: Peter Lang Publishers, pp. 155–65.
Macaulay, T. B. (1835), 'Macaulay's Minute on Education, February 2, 1835'. Online: http://projectsouthasia.sdstate.edu/Docs/history/primary docs/ education/Macaulay001.htm
Mahmood, Syed [1895] (1981), *A History of English Education in India (1781–1893)*, Delhi: Idarahi-i Adabiyat-i Delli.
Mahomet, Dean (1794), *The Travels of Dean Mahomet*, Cork: J. Connor.
'Mantris & Sentries' (1972), *The Current*, 16 September.
Maro Charitra, film, directed by K. Balachander, music director M. S. Viswanathan, India: Andal Productions, 1978.

Mass, film, directed by L. Raghavendra, music director D. S. Prasad, India: Annapurna Studios, 2004.
'Matrimonial', advertisement (1965), *The Indian Express*, 2 October.
McCully, Bruce Tiebout (1966), *English Education and the Origins of Indian Nationalism*, Gloucester, MA: Peter Smith.
Mehrotra, Raja Ram (1998), *Indian English: Texts and Interpretation*, Amsterdam: John Benjamins.
Mehta, Kamal [1976] (1995), 'Rote', in K. Mehta *Delicious Snacks*, Delhi: Hind Pocket Books, p. 15.
Mohan, Ramesh (ed.) (1978), *Indian Writing in English: Papers Read at the Seminar on Indian English held at CIEFL, Hyderabad, July 1972*, Bombay: Orient Longman.
Mr and Mrs Iyer, film, directed by Aparna Sen, music director Ustad Zakir Hussain, India: Triplecom Media Production, 2002.
Mudaliar, A. L. (1960), 'From early times up to the 19th century', in A. L. Mudaliar *Education in India*, Bombay: Asia Publishing House, pp. 1–24.
Mukherjee, Joybrato and Sebastian Hoffmann (2006), 'Describing verb-complementational profiles of New Englishes: A pilot study of Indian English', *English World-Wide* 27:2, 147–73.
Muthiah, S. (1991), *Words in Indian English: A Reader's Guide*, New Delhi: Indus.
Nadkarni, Mangesh (2007), *Beyond Liberal Humanism and Technological Transhumanism*, Delhi: Sri Aurobindo Society.
Nath, Shloka (2007), 'Mumbai school to follow American accent', http://www.ndtv.com/convergence/ndtv/story.aspx?id=NEWEN20070025886, 12 September.
Nelson, Gerald (2007), *International Corpus of English*. Online: http://www.ucl.ac.uk/english-usage/ice/index.htm
News on All India Radio (2006). Online: http://www.newsonair.nic.in/
Nihalani, Paroo, R. K. Tongue, Priya Hosali and Jonathan Crowther [1979] (2005), *Indian and British English: A Handbook of Usage and Pronunciation*, New Delhi: Oxford University Press.
'Nitya Nanda Biswas' jewellery & poddary shop', advertisement (1890), *Amrita Bazar Patrika (Weekly)* 23: 28.
Olavarria de Ersson, Eugenia and Philip Shaw (2003), 'Verb complementation patterns in Indian Standard English', *English World-Wide* 24:2, 137–61.
Pandit, Ira (1986), *Hindi-English Code-switching: Mixed Hindi-English*, Delhi: Datta Book Centre.
Parasher, S. V. (1983), 'Indian English: Certain grammatical, lexical and stylistic features', *English World-Wide* 4:1, 27–42.
Parasher, S. V. (1991), *Indian English: Functions and Form*, New Delhi: Bahri Publications.
Parasher, S. V. (1999a), 'Communication styles in Indian English', in K. V. Tirumalesh (ed.), pp. 16–29.
Parasher, S. V. (1999b), 'Remarks on Indian English', *Indian Linguistics* 60, 121–36.
Patil, Z. N. (1999), 'A once-born literature in a twice-born language: Indianness in Indian English novel', in K. V. Tirumalesh (ed.), pp. 41–58.

Pattanayak, D. P. (1978), 'Some observations on English in India: Its form and function', in Ramesh Mohan (ed.), pp. 184–91.
Pawar, Ranjit (2007), 'In conversation with Lou Hilt', private audio recording, Gurgaon, India, 8 February.
'Perpetual mouse trap' (c.1890), in T. W. J (ed.), p. 132.
Pherwani, Seema (2005), 'Spilling the beans', *Indiantelevision.com*, 18 April. Online: http://us.indiantelevision.com/special/y2k5/kk.htm
Pillai, Sreedhar (2005), 'Take a koffee break', *The Hindu*, 28 May. Online: http://www.thehindu.com/thehindu/mp/2005/05/28/stories/2005052800220300.htm
'Population watch' (2007), *indiastat.com*. Online: http://www.indiastat.com
Prabhakar Babu, B. A. (1971a), *Prosodic Features in Indian English: Stress, Rhythm and Intonation*, post-graduate research diploma project, Hyderabad: CIEFL.
Prabhakar Babu, B. A. (1971b), 'Prosodic features in Indian English: Stress, rhythm and intonation', *CIEFL Bulletin* 8, 33–9.
Prinsep, H. T. (1835), 'Note by H. T. Prinsep, February 15, 1835'. Online: http://projectsouthasia.sdstate.edu/Docs/history/primarydocs/education/HTPrinsep001.htm
Puttuck, W. M. (c. 1890), 'Dear Sir', in T. W. J (ed.), pp. 4–5.
Pyar Kiya to Darna Kya, film, directed by Sohail Khan, music director Jatin and Lalit, India: G. S. Entertainment, 1998.
Rajagopal, V. (2006), 'Ways to make autos safe for passengers', letter to the editor, *Deccan Chronicle*, 15 December.
Rajah, Serfojee (1828), 'Letter from His Highness, the Rajah of Tanjore, to A. D. Campbell', (from Correspondence Respecting Mr. Campbell's Appointment to Tanjore), London: printed by A. Snell, p. 34.
Raja Harischandra, film, directed by D. G. Phalke, India: Phalke Films, 1913.
Ram, Tulsi (1983), *Trading in Language: The Story of English in India*, Delhi: GDK Publications.
Ramaiah, L. S. (1988), *Indian English: A Bibliographical Guide to Resources*, Delhi: Gian Publishing House.
Rangan, Baradwaj (2007), 'Wild bores', *The New Sunday Express*, 11 March.
Rao, Raja [1938] (1974), *Kanthapura*, Madras: Oxford University Press.
Registrar General and Census Commissioner (2007), *Census of India*. Online: http://www.censusindia.gov.in/
'Remarks copied from the visitor's book at an up-country museum' (c. 1890), in T. W. J (ed.), p. 69.
Roach, Peter [1983] (2000), *English Phonetics and Phonology*, Cambridge: Cambridge University Press.
Roy, Rammohun (1999), 'Address to His Excellency the Right Honourable William Pitt, Lord Amherst', in Bruce Carlisle Robertson (ed.), *The Essential Writings of Raja Rammohan Roy*, Delhi: Oxford University Press, pp. 260–3.
Sadanandan, Suchitra (1981), *Stress in Malayalee English: A Generative Phonological Study*, unpublished MLitt. dissertation, Hyderabad: Central Institute of English and Foreign Languages.

Sahgal, Anju and R. K. Agnihotri (1988), 'Indian English phonology: A sociolinguistic perspective', *English World-Wide* 9:1, 51–64.
Sand, Andrea (2004), 'Shared morpho-syntactic features in contact varieties of English: Article use', *World Englishes* 23:2, 281–98.
Santanagopalan, Nagalakshmi (2007), 'Legend of the cherry blossoms', *The Hindu, Young World*, 2 March.
Sanyal, Jyoti (2006), *Indlish: The Book for Every English-speaking Indian*, New Delhi: Viva Books Private Limited.
'Saturdays are real fun' (2006), *Deccan Chronicle*, 28 March.
Satya (2007), *The Publishing Horizon*. Online: http://prayatna.typepad.com/publishing/country_markets/index.html
Schneider, Edgar W. (2004), 'How to trace structural nativization: Particle verbs in world Englishes', *World Englishes* 23:2, 227–49.
Sengupta, Indira Chowdhury (1996), 'A supplement of Indian English', in A. S. Hornby, *Oxford Advanced Learner's Dictionary of Current English*, Oxford: Oxford University Press, pp. 1429–75.
Serjeantson, Mary S. (1935), *A History of Foreign Words in English*, London: Routledge & Kegan Paul.
Sethi, J (1980), 'Word accent in educated Panjabi-speakers' English', *CIEFL Bulletin* XVI:2, 31–55.
Shah, A. B. (1968), *The Great Debate: Language Controversy and University Education*, Bombay: Lalvani.
Sharma, Devyani (2005), 'Transfer and universals in Indian English article use', *Studies in Second Language Acquisition* 27:4, 535–66.
Shastri, S.V (1988), 'Kolhapur corpus of Indian English and work done on its basis so far', *ICAME Journal* 12, 15–26.
Shastri, S. V., C. T. Patil Kulkarni and Geetha S. Shastri (1986), *Manual of Information to Accompany the Kolhapur Corpus of Indian English for use with Digital Computers*, Kolhapur: Department of English, Shivaji University.
Shrivastava, Bhuma (2006), 'Google Book Search seeking partners in India', *rediff.com*. Online: http://www.rediff.com///money/2006/sep/20google.htm
Shuja, Asif (1995), *Urdu-English Phonetics and Phonology*, New Delhi: Bahri Publications.
'Shuttle camp in full swing' (2007), *Deccan Chronicle*, 22 March.
Singh, Rajendra (1985), 'Grammatical constraints on code-mixing: Evidence from Hindi-English', *The Canadian Journal of Linguistics* 30:1, 33–45.
Singh, Rajendra (1995), 'We, they and us: A note on code-switching and stratification in North India', in Rajendra Singh, Probal Dasgupta and Jayant K. Lele (eds), *Explorations in Indian Socio-linguistics*, New Delhi: Sage Publications, pp. 131–4.
Sinha, Surendra Prasad (1978), *English in India: A Historical Study with Particular Reference to English Education in India*, Patna: Janaki Prakashan.
Sonntag, Selma K. (2000), 'Ideology and policy in the politics of the English language in North India', in Thomas Ricento (ed.), *Ideology, Politics and Language Policies: Focus on English*, Amsterdam: John Benjamins Publishing Company, pp. 133–49.

Soob Row, Vennelacunty (1873), *The Life of Vennelacunty Soob Row, (native of Ongole), Translator and Interpreter of the Late Sudr Court, Madras, from 1815 to 1829 as Written by himself*, Madras: Vennelacunty Venkata Gopal Row.
'South Asian arts' (2007), in *Encyclopaedia Britannica*. Online: http://search.eb.com/eb/article-65263
Sreetilak, S. (2007), *Fiction in Films, Films in Fiction: The Making of New English India*, New Delhi: Viva Books Private Limited.
Sridhar, Kamal K. (1989), *English in Indian Bilingualism*, New Delhi: Manohar.
Srihari, Gudipoodi (2007), 'An expressive concert', *The Hindu*, 20 April.
Stewart, Ralph (2003), 'A decline in spoken English?', *English Today* 75, 19:3, 57–8.
Stocqueler, J. H. (1920), *The Oriental Interpreter and Treasury of East India Knowledge: A Companion to "The Handbook of British India"*, London: C. Cox.
Strevens, Peter (1972), *British and American English*, London: Collier-Macmillan Publishers.
Subba Rao, G. (1954), *Indian Words in English: A Study in Indo-British Cultural and Linguistic Relations*, London: Oxford University Press.
Subramanian, K. (1978), 'Penchant for the florid', in Ramesh Mohan (ed.), pp. 203–6.
Suman, Mickey (2007), *An Acceptability Study of Hinglish*, unpublished MPhil dissertation, University of Hyderabad.
Swaminathan, K. (1975), *Ramana Maharshi*, Delhi: National Book Trust, India.
'Teachers & Professors', advertisement (2007), *Free Ads Weekly* 11:28.
Tharoor, Shashi (1989), *The Great Indian Novel*, New Delhi: Penguin Books.
The most stolen magazine of the century, advertisement (1972), *The Current*, 9 September.
36, Chowringhee Lane, film, directed by Aparna Sen, music director Vanraj Bhatia, India: Film-Valas Company, 1981.
Thirumalai, M. S. (2004), 'Language policy in the formative years of Indian National Congress: 1885–1905', *Language in India*, 4 (10 October). Online: http://www.languageinindia.com/oct2004/languagepolicyearlycongress2.html
Thundy, Zacharias (1976), 'The origins of Indian English', *CIEFL Bulletin* 12, 29–40.
Tirumalesh, K. V. (1990), 'Indian English', in K.V. Tirumalesh *Derrida's Heel of Achilles and Other Essays*, Delhi: Bahri Publications, pp. 44–6.
Tirumalesh, K. V. (ed.) (1999), *Language Matters: Essays on Language, Literature and Translation*, New Delhi: Allied Publishers Limited.
'To let,' advertisement (1875), *The Hindoo Patriot*, 11 January.
Trevelyan, Charles E. (1838), *On the Education of the People of India*, London: Green and Longmans.
Trivedi, Vithaldas G. (1924), *Annual Report: Year 1923–24, Watson Museum of Antiquities, Rajkot*, 1–8.
Trudgill, Peter and Jean Hannah (2002), *International English: A Guide to Varieties of Standard English*, London: Arnold.

Trudgill, Peter, Terttu Nevalainen and Ilse Wischer (2002), 'Dynamic *have* in North American and British Isles English', *English Language and Linguistics* 6:1, 1–15.
Tulpule, Aparna (1994), 'Bridging tongues,' letter to the editor, *Indian Review of Books* 3:5, p. 39.
Valentine, Tamara M. (1991), 'Getting the message across: Discourse markers in Indian English', *World Englishes* 10:3, 325–34.
Verma, S. K. (1978), 'Syntactic irregularities in Indian English', in Ramesh Mohan (ed.), pp. 207–20.
Vijayakrishnan, K. G. (1978), *Stress in Tamilian English: A Study within the Framework of Generative Phonology*, unpublished MLitt dissertation, Hyderabad: Central Institute of English and Foreign Languages.
Vivekananda, Swami (1985), 'Why we disagree', in Swami Vivekananda *Abridged Edition of the Complete Works of Swami Vivekananda*, Calcutta: Advaita Ashrama, pp. 2–3.
W. D. (c. 1890), 'Complainant against a fellow workman', in T. W. J (ed.), p. 3.
Whitworth, George Clifford (1907), *Indian English: An Examination of the Errors of Idiom made by Indians in Writing English*, Lechtworth: Garden City Press.
Whitworth, George Clifford [1885] (1976), *An Anglo-Indian Dictionary: A Glossary of Indian Terms used in English, and of such English or other Non-Indian Terms as have obtained special meanings in India*, London: Kegan Paul, Trench & Co.
Wilson, Andrew (2005), 'Modal verbs in written Indian English: A quantitative and comparative analysis of the Kolhapur corpus using correspondence analysis', *ICAME Journal* 29, 151–69.
Wilson, Horace Hayman [1855] (1968), *A Glossary of Judicial and Revenue Terms and of Useful Words Occurring in Official Documents Relating to the Administration of the Government of British India*, Delhi: Munshiram Manoharlal.
Wiltshire, Caroline R. (2005), 'The "Indian English" of Tibeto-Burman language speakers', *English World-Wide* 26:3, 275–300.
Wiltshire, Caroline and James D. Harnsberger (2006), 'The influence of Gujarati and Tamil L1s on Indian English: A preliminary study', *World Englishes* 25:1, 91–104.
Wiltshire, Caroline and Russell Moon (2003), 'Phonetic stress in Indian English vs. American English', *World Englishes* 22:3, 291–303.
Wright, Arnold (1891), *Baboo English as 'Tis Writ: Being Curiosities of Indian Journalism*, London: T. Fisher Unwin.
Yadurajan, K. S. (2001), *Current English: A Guide for the User of English in India*, New Delhi: Oxford University Press.
Yule, Henry (2006), *Digital Dictionaries of South Asia*. Online: http://dsal.uchicago.edu/dictionaries/hobsonjobson/
Yule, Henry and A. C. Burnell [1886] (1986), *Hobson-Jobson: A Glossary of Colloquial Anglo-Indian Words and Phrases, and of Kindred Terms, Etymological, Historical, Geographical and Discursive*, New Delhi: Rupa & Co.

Index

acrolect, 14
adjective, 32, 43, 76, 126
adverb, 50, 55, 126
adverbial, 53, 54
AE, 13, 33, 39, 41–2, 44, 50–1, 63–4, 66–7, 78, 121, 125
affixation, 76, 80, 82
AIR *see* All India Radio
All India Radio, 7, 11, 18, 19, 25
alveolar flap, 20
alveolar sounds, 21, 22
American English *see* AE
Anglicist, 105, 106, 107, 130
Anglicist-Orientalist debate, 103, 104–6, 129
Anglicist-Vernacularist conflict, 104
Anglo-Indian, 8, 15, 16n, 128
Anglophones, 15
arts, 6, 7, 9, 10, 12, 73
Asiatic Society, 100
attitudes, 41, 122, 123

basilect, 14
BE, 14, 33, 39, 40–2, 43–4, 50–1, 63–4, 66–7, 69, 72, 78, 84, 85, 127
Bengal, 8, 9, 81, 96, 100, 109, 111, 112
Bengali
  language, 1, 2, 4, 9, 70, 148
  people, 9, 22, 81
Bentinck, Lord William, 106
bisyllabic word *see* disyllabic word
Bollywood, 10, 11, 12, 118
Bombay, 9, 10, 11, 16n, 18, 47, 79, 95, 98, 99, 104, 105, 107, 129, 147, 148

British English *see* BE
Brown Corpus, 66, 131

Calcutta, 9, 16n, 18, 81, 95, 96, 98, 99, 100, 101, 103, 104, 105, 108, 109, 129
casual speech, 37
census, 2, 3, 15n, 40
cinema *see* film
circumlocution, 90
clear l, 23
cline
  of bilingualism, 14, 15
  of proficiency, 15, 18, 39, 115
  of pronunciation, 18
code-mixing, 85, 118, 123, 131
code-switching, 8, 62, 63, 65n, 75, 80, 91, 92
collective noun, 53
collocation, 113, 126, 127
Commission, 5, 107, 108, 112, 129
conjunctions, 85
Constitution, 4, 5, 6, 11, 111, 118

dark l, 23
dental plosives, 21
dialect, 2, 12, 40, 87, 110, 123, 156, 157
diglossic situation, 6
discourse, 50, 62, 63, 66, 85, 86, 91, 94, 115, 126, 130, 158
distancing language, 92
disyllabic words, 26, 27, 30, 60
Doordarshan, 11, 83

Dravidian, 2, 23, 24, 30, 31, 36, 38n, 74, 90, 124
dual sets, 75

East India Company, 95, 96, 98, 100, 101, 102, 103, 105, 112, 115, 130, 134
-*ed*, 79
educated Indian English, 14, 123
educated Indian Pronunciation, 18
education, 5, 6, 37, 97, 98, 100, 101, 103, 104, 105, 112, 129, 130
  higher, 106, 108, 129
  occupational, 108
  primary, 108
  secondary, 112
  see also English education
elision, 45
Elphinstone, Lord, 104
English education, 12, 87, 95, 101–3, 104–6, 107–8, 124, 129, 130
English medium, 100
English newspapers, 4, 143
euphemisms, 88

film, 6, 7, 8, 10, 11, 12, 13, 15n, 20, 29, 42, 50, 52, 53, 63, 65, 68, 78, 81, 92, 144
first language, 5, 10, 15, 22, 40
formal speech, 75

Gandhi, M. K., 108, 110, 111, 142
geminate, 26, 27
generalised IE, 18, 22, 124
Germanic word, 46
Goa, 7, 96, 97, 129
grammatical classes, 128
Grant, Charles, 101, 103, 105, 129
Gujarati
  language, 1, 2, 9, 22, 148
  people, 36, 136

Hastings, Warren, 101, 103, 129
have, 41, 48, 49, 51, 63, 64, 65n, 88, 91
head, 78, 80, 127

Hindi
  language, 1, 2, 3–5, 9, 11–12, 13, 15n, 22, 29, 62, 73, 74, 75, 86, 87, 92, 94n, 111, 112, 118, 126, 127, 130, 142, 143, 153, 157
  speakers, 22
Hindi-English, 8, 62, 63, 85
Hindustani, 7, 9, 70, 71, 73, 109, 111, 127, 130
Hinglish, 118
Hobson-Jobson, 72, 80, 128
Hunter, Sir Wilson, 108, 129
hybrid constructions, 80, 81–2, 127
hybrid items *see* hybrid constructions
hybrid words *see* hybrid constructions

idioms, 53, 61–2, 90–1, 113, 127
independence, 1, 95, 97, 106, 108, 109, 110, 111, 129, 130
India Act, 100
Indian Recommended Pronunciation, 127
Indian variety of English, 14, 39, 127
  non-standard, 20, 25, 29, 37, 40, 88
  standard, 14, 17, 18, 20, 23, 39, 78
Indians' English, 13, 123
Indo-Aryan, 1, 2, 21, 30, 36, 38n, 90, 124
informal speech, 45, 48, 57, 75
-*ing*, 48, 79
intelligibility, 124
inter-clausal tense agreement, 49
intermediate accent, 17
International Corpus of English, 43, 131
intonation, 34–6, 58

Kashmiri, 22
Kolhapur Corpus, 66, 131

Lancaster-Oslo/Bergen Corpus, 66, 131
language family, 1, 2, 36, 124; *see also* Dravidian, Indo-Aryan
language policy, 5
linker, 85
literature, 6, 7, 12–13, 96, 105, 106, 107, 118, 120, 122, 133–7

Macaulay, T. B., 95, 97, 106, 118, 129, 130
Madras, 9, 16n, 18, 95, 97, 98, 99, 105, 107, 111, 113, 129, 139, 141
Mahomet, Dean, 12, 101, 133–4
Malayalam
  language, 2, 23, 70, 98, 148
  speakers, 25
Marathi
  language, 1, 2, 9, 22, 70
  speakers, 148
medium of instruction, 98, 104, 106
mesolect, 14
missionary, 15n, 98, 100, 101, 105, 107
modals, 50–1, 90
modifier, 80, 84, 127
modulect, 123
movie *see* film
music, 7–9, 73, 80, 135, 136
  fusion, 7
  Hindustani, 7
  Karnatic, 7, 145
  popular, 7–8, 9, 80

national language, 109, 111, 148
native language, 2, 4, 12, 14, 15, 18, 31, 40, 90, 112
native variety, 21, 31, 34, 39, 40, 41, 44, 47, 49, 50, 52, 58, 59, 64, 66, 68, 69, 72, 77, 78, 84, 123, 126
nearness language, 92
Nehru, Jawaharlal, 111
neutralised, 20, 24, 25
news channels, 33, 88
non-native variety, 39, 52, 122, 126
non-rhotic accent, 19–20, 25, 37
non-standard accents *see* non-standard pronunciation
non-standard pronunciation, 25, 27, 35
norm, 18, 55, 117, 124, 141

off, 47, 48, 144, 145, 148
official language, 4, 5, 111
Official Languages Act, 4, 112
Orientalist, 103, 104, 105, 106, 129
Oriya, 2, 22
out, 48,142

past participle form, 63
Patois, 96, 98
pidgins, 95, 96, 112
  Baboo English, Babu English, 14, 112–13, 131, 132, 139, 150, 152
  Boxwallah English, 112
  Butler English, 13, 112, 113–14
  poetry, 12, 36, 136, 148
Portugal, 96, 97, 98
Portuguese
  language, 69, 70, 96, 97, 98, 99
  people, 7, 15n, 96, 97, 98
prepositions, 46, 61
present perfect aspect, 49
Presidency, 95, 98, 100, 101, 104, 105, 107, 108, 113, 129
prestige marker, 19
Prinsep, H. T., 105, 106, 129
proficiency, 15, 18, 19, 48, 52, 86, 106, 122, 133
prosody, 36
publications, 3–4
Punjabi, 2, 29, 62

Raj, 9, 72, 98
Received Pronunciation *see* RP
regional differences, 10
regional equivalents, 22
regional variation, 17, 22, 37
register, 71, 73, 76
retroflexion, 21, 23, 37, 158
rhetorical device, 57
rhotic accent, 20, 25, 27, 37
rhythm, 33, 34
Romance vocabulary, 46, 93
Romance words *see* Romance vocabulary
Roy, Raja Rammohun, 103, 105, 106
RP, 17, 18, 19, 20, 22, 23, 24, 25, 26, 27, 28–9, 31, 32, 33, 38, 121

Sanskrit, 11, 12, 15n, 69, 70, 71, 74, 104, 105, 111, 121
script, 97, 148
second language, 3, 6, 14, 15, 17, 18, 39
semantic changes, 69, 128
sentence stress, 32–3

SIEP, 19–22, 23, 24–6, 27, 29–30, 31–2, 33, 34, 36, 37, 156, 157, 158
standard English, 13, 14, 48, 56, 88, 133, 134, 140
Standard IE Pronunciation *see* SIEP
standard Indian English, 40, 42, 76, 125, 133
suffixes, 28–9, 79, 80, 81
syllabification, 30, 124
syllable weight, 30

tag questions, 59, 88–90, 125, 126
  isn't it?, 59, 88–9, 93
  no?, 59, 88, 89, 93, 136
talk shows, 11, 12
Tamil
  language, 2, 9, 21, 22, 23, 25, 70, 71, 74, 86, 87, 98, 111, 114, 148
  people, 21, 23, 36, 81
television, 7, 10, 11, 12, 33, 63
Telugu
  language, 2, 8, 11, 24, 25, 52, 62, 65, 71, 86, 92, 105, 148
  people, 111, 148
theatre, 7, 9, 10, 150

three-language formula, 112
tone *see* intonation
topicalisation, 53, 125
tune *see* intonation
trisyllabic words, 30

universities, 10, 67, 108
Urdu, 1, 2, 9, 62, 74, 127, 148
Urdu-English, 35

verb, 32, 43–9, 54, 56, 57, 58, 63, 64, 65, 77, 126, 146, 151
  complement, 43–6, 55, 153
  ditransitive, 43–5
  intransitive, 43, 45, 48
  transitive, 43, 45, 47, 77
verbal derivative, 78
vernacularists, 107
vernaculars, 98, 104, 105, 108

weak forms, 33, 34
wh-questions, 35, 56, 57, 126
Wood, Charles, 108, 129

yes-no questions, 35, 58

EU representative:
Easy Access System Europe
Mustamäe tee 50, 10621 Tallinn, Estonia
Gpsr.requests@easproject.com

www.ingramcontent.com/pod-product-compliance
Lightning Source LLC
Chambersburg PA
CBHW051812230426
43672CB00012B/2701